REACHING FOR

THE SAVIOR

REACHING FOR THE SAVIOR

REYNA I. ABURTO

DESERET
BOOK

Salt Lake City, Utah

Library of Congress Cataloging-in-Publication Data

Names: Aburto, Reyna I., 1963– author.
Title: Reaching for the Savior / Reyna I. Aburto.
Description: Salt Lake City, Utah : Deseret Book, [2021] | Includes bibliographical references. | Summary: "Drawing upon her unique life experiences, Sister Reyna Aburto, Second Counselor in the Relief Society of The Church of Jesus Christ of Latter-day Saints, invites readers to join with her in strengthening Christ's Church"—Provided by publisher.
Identifiers: LCCN 2020044987 | ISBN 9781629728728 (hardback)
Subjects: LCSH: Jesus Christ—Mormon interpretations. | The Church of Jesus Christ of Latter-day Saints—Doctrines. | Christian life—Mormon authors. | Mormon Church—Doctrines.
Classification: LCC BX8656 .A28 2021 | DDC 232.088/2893—dc23
LC record available at https://lccn.loc.gov/2020044987

Printed in the United States of America
Lake Book Manufacturing, Inc., Melrose Park, IL

10 9 8 7 6 5 4 3 2 1

With love to my husband Carlos,
my ancestors, and my posterity;
as well as to any person looking for the peace
and healing that Jesus Christ offers us
through His redeeming Atonement.

CONTENTS

REACHING FOR THE SAVIOR

A story is told about two brothers who were extremely lazy. Their father was a farmer who worked tirelessly for long hours to maintain his farm. Even though he tried to teach the principle of hard work to his sons, they did not want to live up to his example and instruction and took every opportunity to avoid doing their chores.

One day, the two brothers were, as usual, steering clear from working at all costs and went to their favorite hiding place. One of them was lying facedown on the grass and the other one was lying faceup, right next to him. The one that was looking up saw something up in the sky for the first time. A huge plane was passing above their small town. With the desire to share that impressive sight with his brother, he exclaimed: "Look! In the sky! I have never seen anything like that before! It must be a plane! It is amazing!" Without moving or even turning one inch, and still lying facedown, his brother replied, "Lucky you that you can see it!" He was too lazy to even turn around and look up!

This story reminds me of the time when fiery serpents bit the children of Israel while they were in the desert, and many of these people died. They begged Moses to pray to the Lord to protect them from the serpents. When Moses did so, the Lord told him to make a fiery serpent out of brass, to set it on a pole, and to instruct those who had been bitten to look at it, so they could live (see Numbers 21:6–9).

During His earthly ministry, the Lord Jesus Christ clarified that the serpent on the pole was a symbol of Himself: "As Moses lifted up the serpent in the wilderness, even so must the Son of man be lifted up: That whosoever believeth in him should not perish, but have eternal life" (John 3:14–15).

I love the further insights we get from the Book of Mormon. Nephi explained that the Lord "prepared a way that they might be healed; and the labor which they had to perform was to look; and because of the simpleness of the way, or the easiness of it, there were many who perished" (1 Nephi 17:41).

Alma also expanded on these truths when he said: "But few understood the meaning of those things, and because of the hardness of their hearts. But there were many who were so hardened that they would not look, therefore they perished. Now the reason they would not look is because they did not believe that it would heal them" (Alma 33:20).

According to these passages of scripture, many of the people of Israel did not look at the serpent on the pole in order to be healed because it was such a simple thing to do that they did not believe it had power to heal them. Due to their unbelief or maybe to their "spiritual laziness," they did not make even the smallest effort to look. Does that sound like the story of the two brothers? Could it also describe us when we refuse to reach up to the Savior by doing the simple things that turn our hearts to Him?

As we go through our mortal existence, sometimes we find ourselves amid tribulation and sorrow. We experience heart-wrenching situations, and it becomes hard to find the strength to go on. During those times, it may be difficult to believe that when we reach for the Savior and turn our hearts to Him, He has the power to heal us.

Other times, we have periods of spiritual laziness in our souls. We just go through the motions and are not "anxiously engaged" in reaching up to God so we can receive help from Him (D&C 58:27).

I grew up as a Catholic, and even though I believed in God, I did not have a clear understanding of His nature and His love for me. I believed in Jesus Christ but did not truly comprehend how much I needed Him in my life and that I had to be more proactive in reaching up to Him in order to be saved through His grace. I was in some sort of "spiritual sleep" and was "spiritually lazy," without the desire to exert any kind of effort to reach up to heaven for help or direction in my life.

It was not until I was twenty-six years old that I "came to [myself]" (Luke 15:17), like the prodigal son. At that point, I had just gone through a painful final separation from my first husband; I had a three-year-old-son, Xavier, whom I loved with all my heart; and I found myself overwhelmed by fear, despair, and hopelessness. It was then, through the Light of Christ, that I received a testimony of the restored gospel of Jesus Christ. I felt the sincere desire to join The Church of Jesus Christ of Latter-day Saints and to start participating in this remarkable journey of discipleship, experiencing its ups and downs, just like everyone else.

All I needed was to have a desire to reach for the Savior, turn my heart to Him, believe in Him, and act on that belief. At that time, I was not physically lazy—I was busy and working hard to provide for myself and my son—but I was going through a long period of spiritual laziness, without stretching myself toward God.

It was actually a simple act of faith—of reaching up— performed by a fourteen-year-old that started the glorious process of the Restoration of the gospel in this "dispensation of the fulness of times" (D&C 128:18). As we know, at that young age, Joseph Smith found himself "in the midst of [a] war of words and tumult of opinions" (Joseph Smith—History 1:10). Does that sound like the times in which we live? Don't we sometimes feel surrounded by a wave of "stirring, division, and contention"? (vv. 5–6). At times, there are so many things competing for our attention, for our time, and even for our hearts, that it may be hard to keep our sight on the Lord and His gospel.

Young Joseph often asked himself, "What is to be done?" (Joseph Smith—History 1:10). It is significant that he not only wanted to know the truth, but he also wanted to know what he needed to *do*. He was willing to find out what God's will was for him and to act on it.

The first answer he received entered his heart with great force as he was reading in James 1:5: "If any of you lack wisdom, let him ask of God, that giveth to all men liberally, and upbraideth not; and it shall be given him."

Joseph decided to act on those feelings. He chose a time and a place where he could exercise his faith and have a personal conversation with God. After going to the place he had chosen, he began to pour out his soul to his Creator. Then, an astonishing force overcame him entirely, in such a way that he could not speak. However, he exerted *all his powers* to call upon God. It was then that he saw a pillar of light "above the brightness of the sun," descending gradually until it fell upon him, and he had the glorious experience of seeing "God, the Eternal Father, and . . . His Son, Jesus Christ" (Articles of Faith 1:1), who not only answered his question but also gave him instructions on what to do (see Joseph Smith—History 1:5–20). Our membership in the Church is among the fruits of Joseph's action of reaching up to God. Our process of reaching, like his, begins with desire but quickly turns to action.

In his April 2017 general conference talk, President Russell M. Nelson said that in order to "[draw] the Savior's power into our lives [we need] to reach up to Him in faith. [And] such reaching requires diligent, focused effort."

He then talked about "the woman who suffered for twelve years with a debilitating problem [and] exercised great faith in the Savior, exclaiming, 'If I may touch but his clothes, I shall be whole' (Mark 5:28).

"This faithful, focused woman needed to stretch as far as she could to access His power. Her physical stretching was symbolic of her spiritual stretching."

President Nelson added: "Many of us have cried out from the depths of our hearts a variation of this woman's words: 'If I could spiritually stretch enough to draw the Savior's power into my life, I would know how to handle my heart-wrenching situation. I would know what to do. And I would have the power to do it.'"[1]

No matter our circumstances, we all need to draw the Savior's power into our life at all times. We all should strive to have a clear understanding of our divine nature and purpose so that each decision we make in life can be guided by our desire to receive virtue and healing from the Savior. We all can constantly exert all our powers, stretch ourselves physically and spiritually, and reach for the Savior so our afflictions can be "swallowed up in [His] joy" (Alma 31:38). To attain that, we can start with the desire to draw closer to Him, nurturing that desire and exerting all our powers, until desire becomes faith and belief in the power that He has to help and to heal us.

Exerting all our powers in simple ways could mean to constantly pray to our Heavenly Father, knowing that He is our Father, that He knows our hearts, that He listens to our prayers, and that He truly wants us to be happy in this life and throughout eternity.

It could also mean to focus our thoughts on the Savior in a more intentional way. It may seem too simple, but I testify that turning our minds and hearts to our Savior as we go about our daily routines is a powerful way to reach up to Him and to draw from His power.

Another way to exert all our powers could be by reaching up to Heavenly Father through a diligent, personal study of the scriptures. Sometimes the difference between tapping into the Gospel Library and any other app on our phone is just a matter of a few millimeters. Just a simple and easy movement shows our desire to reach for the Savior—and to receive His light and guidance.

The same principle applies to studying the words of the living prophets, seers, and revelators. From our called leaders, we receive a wealth of inspired counsel. We have all of these gifts of knowledge and wisdom at our fingertips, literally.

A significant way in which we exerted all our powers and showed the Savior that we wanted to receive virtue from Him was when we went into the waters of baptism to make a covenant with God, promising Him that we would obey His commandments.

That act of faith required a spiritual and physical effort from us and from the people who supported us in our decision to be a disciple of Christ.

Every Sunday we have the opportunity to stretch out our hand as we make the decision to partake of the sacrament, renew all of the covenants we have made with God, and make a new covenant with Him. Through that simple and regular act of stretching and reaching up to the Savior, acknowledging that we need His help at all times, we receive the strength and the vision we need every day of our week.

In the modern world, many of us have a busy life. We are anxiously engaged in school, work, Church callings, helping family and friends, and having a social life. We may not be physically lazy. But we should be careful not to fall into the trap of spiritual laziness and keep doing the "small and simple things" (Alma 37:6) that will get us closer to the Savior so He can bless us.

President Nelson also counseled:

"When you reach up for the Lord's power in your life with the same intensity that a drowning person has when grasping and gasping for air, power from Jesus Christ will be yours. When the Savior knows you truly want to reach up to Him—when He can feel that the greatest desire of your heart is to draw His power into your life—you will be led by the Holy Ghost to know exactly what you should do.

"When you spiritually stretch beyond anything you have ever done before, then His power will flow into you."[2]

The Lord has promised us that when we reach, He responds, explaining with these beautiful words, "Draw near unto me and I will draw near unto you; seek me diligently and ye shall find me; ask, and ye shall receive; knock, and it shall be opened unto you" (D&C 88:63).

Together with Alma, I pledge to you: "O my brethren [and sisters], if ye could be healed by merely casting about your eyes that ye might be healed, would ye not behold quickly, or would ye rather harden your hearts in unbelief, and be slothful, that ye would not cast about your eyes, that ye might perish? . . . Then cast about your eyes and begin to believe in the Son of God, that he will come to redeem his people, and that he shall suffer and die to atone for their sins; and that he shall rise again from the dead, which shall bring to pass the resurrection, that all men shall stand before him, to be judged at the last and judgment day, according to their works" (Alma 33:21–22).

I know that we have a Father in Heaven, who loves us and knows each of us personally. I know that our Lord Jesus Christ is the Son of God, the Only Begotten Son, the Prince of Peace, and that He has the power and the desire to heal us, and to embrace us in His loving arms as we go through this mortal life. He loves each of us, He knows each of us, He wants us to draw near unto Him, and "from His perspective, [we are] not that far away."[3] He has sent us the Comforter, even the Spirit of truth, who testifies to us of the saving and enabling power that comes from Jesus Christ, our Savior and Redeemer.

WE CAN REACH FOR THE SAVIOR WHEN
WE EXERT ALL OUR POWERS AND STRETCH
OURSELVES IN SIMPLE BUT SIGNIFICANT
WAYS TO CONSTANTLY COME UNTO HIM.

NOTES

1. Russell M. Nelson, "Drawing the Power of Jesus Christ into Our Lives," *Ensign,* May 2017, 41–42.
2. Russell M. Nelson, "Drawing the Power of Jesus Christ into Our Lives," 42.
3. Henry B. Eyring, "My Peace I Leave with You," *Ensign,* May 2017, 18.

HIS BIRTH, OUR LIFE

In December 1972, I was nine years old and lived in Managua, Nicaragua, with my parents, my ten-year-old brother, Noel (who went by Noelito), and my three-month-old sister, Sandra. My aunt and my little cousin lived next door. Our family was Catholic by tradition, and we would attend mass occasionally.

My brother Noelito and I were close—both in age and in every other aspect. He was always by my side, protecting me, holding my hand before crossing the street as we walked to school. I do not remember ever quarreling or competing with him. He was my brother and my friend.

In December, the holiday excitement could be felt everywhere. The window displays in the stores reminded us that Christmas was around the corner. Bright lights of all colors gave a magical touch to every street and every home.

Our Christmas tree was up, with shining red spheres hung from the branches and tiny lights that made the tree look much bigger than it was. Under the tree, we had a Nativity set as a symbol for us of the reason we celebrated Christmas. All the figures were in place: Joseph, Mary, the shepherds, and the animals. All were there except for one: *el Niño Dios*, or Baby Jesus.

In Nicaragua, we had the tradition of getting together with our extended family on Christmas Eve. We shared a delicious meal, the adults had a lively conversation, and the children were excited, knowing that at midnight, when Baby Jesus was born, He would bring us presents, which magically appeared under the Christmas tree. Fireworks would be lit all over the city, announcing the birth of our Savior. Then, we would reverently set Him in the Nativity set, because He had finally been born.

Doing this ritual every year gave me a sense of awe and gratitude toward Him. Baby Jesus was the one who brought me all my Christmas presents, and as I learned later, He is the source of all righteousness and the one who gives us eternal life. He was born to bring "great joy" to all of us, to "bring redemption unto the world, to save the world from sin" (3 Nephi 9:21).

That particular year, I had been counting the days for Christmas to arrive. I had been more anxious than in previous years. It may have been because I was nine years old. I was old enough to know exactly what would happen, and at the same time, young enough that I was still immersed in the magic of the season.

On the night of December 22, I got ready for bed, excited that Christmas Eve was just two days ahead. Noelito's bed was right next to mine and we both shared the anticipation. I closed my eyes with a big smile, with the assurance that the long-awaited day was getting closer and closer.

In the middle of the night, I started having what felt like a strange nightmare. It was pitch dark and it smelled like loose dirt. I tried to sit up, but my legs were trapped. I felt a heavy weight on them. I reached out with my hands and could touch something over me. I was not sure what was happening. I tried to listen, and I heard a woman screaming, asking for help. Her voice sounded distant. I followed her lead and started yelling, begging for someone to help me.

The earth would tremble here and there, and when that happened, I stayed quiet, trying to listen to my surroundings. After some time, my screams were heard. I felt movement over me and heard voices getting closer. They asked me, "Are you there?" I answered, "Yes, I'm here." After several minutes, I saw some faces. I was being rescued by my neighbors. They lifted me up and carried me. My mother was with them, and I realized that she was the woman who had been screaming all that time.

They took me out to the street, and I sat there in the total darkness. Everything looked different. My father was lying down next to me. He was hurt and unable to help my mother, who, after making sure that I was fine, went back to the rubble to keep looking for our other family members. Our neighbor from the house across the street was holding my baby sister.

After some time, a neighbor brought Noelito to the street. He placed my brother close to me and pronounced, "He is dead." My father started crying, my mother was in shock, and I wished I could wake up from that bad dream. It was hard for my mind to grasp the reality of what was happening.

Then I realized that our house was also gone. We had lost our home and all our possessions. We had lost everything—our furniture, our clothes, all that we owned. All I had left were the clothes I was wearing: a T-shirt and shorts. In my mind, I pictured my family as beggars on the street, asking for money to get something to eat. A 6.3-magnitude earthquake had shaken the country, killing about 10,000 people, injuring nearly 20,000, and displacing another 300,000.

Later that night, my cousins who lived a few blocks away came to see how we were doing. They were in their late teens, and I had always looked up to them. Seeing them gave me comfort. My mother asked them to take me to their home. It felt good to see my aunt, uncle, grandmother, and the rest of my cousins. Their home was still standing but was severely damaged, so we could not go inside. I fell asleep on their sidewalk.

When I opened my eyes, the sun was already up. One of my cousins, who also had a baby herself, was holding my baby sister. My cousins explained to me that my parents had gone to the cemetery to bury my brother and my baby cousin Elena, who had also died.

My aunt's neighbors had a huge backyard, and they let us stay there. It was like a camp with beds everywhere. We got water and bags of food from big trucks that went around the city. We all shared the food.

That night, I lay down on a makeshift bed in the backyard and looked up. The sky was full of stars, and it was hard to fall asleep, but I finally did. When the sun was up, the next morning, my aunt came to me and gave me a present. I was confused—I did not know why she was giving me a gift. I asked her, "Why are you giving me this present? Is it my birthday?"

She answered, "No, today is Christmas Eve."

I had forgotten all about it. How could I forget about Christmas when I had been waiting for it so anxiously? At that moment, reality hit me, and sadness overwhelmed me. Was it true that my brother was gone? Would I ever wake up from this nightmare? Couldn't I just go back to my normal life and forget about all of this? It was too much to take in. I started crying for the first time since the earthquake because I could not make sense of it all.

I was not yet a member of The Church of Jesus Christ of Latter-day Saints. I did not know about the plan of salvation. I just knew that Noelito was dead. I thought that he was probably in heaven, but I did not know exactly what had happened to him. I wondered if I was ever going to be able to see him again. I remember having that question and that longing in my heart: "What happened to him? Where is he? Where did he go? Will I see him again?"

Now I realize that as a young girl, I had the desire to know about God's plan of salvation. I wanted to know where we come from, what is the purpose of our life, and what happens to us after we die. Don't we all have those yearnings when we lose a loved one or when we go through difficulties in our life? We are all in need of the assurance that our life has a purpose and that there is something to hope for. At some point or another, the realities of life make us pause, stop focusing on our routine, look up, and have a broader perspective of our existence. Those moments of reflection help us understand who we really are as children of God, how much we depend on Him, and how much we need each other.

When I was eleven years old, my mother had a baby boy who was named Henry. He was a reason for joy for us, but life was still hard. Sometimes we would be sitting in the living room and my mother would start crying out of nowhere. I knew that she was hurting inside because she did not know exactly what had happened to my brother Noelito.

Around that time, I started having a daydream in which I would see Noelito come and knock on our door. I would open the door, he would be standing right there, and he would tell me, "Guess what? I am not dead. I am alive. I was somewhere else, but I was not allowed to come to you. But now I can come to you. I will stay with you, and I will never leave again." That daydream helped me cope with the pain and the sorrow that I felt for losing him.

This thought came to my mind over and over. I wanted with all my heart for it to be true. It was still hard for me to accept that Noelito was gone. I wanted it to happen so badly that sometimes I would just sit in our living room staring at the door, hoping that he would come and that I would see him again.

I moved to San Francisco, California, when I was twenty-one, after feeling the urge to leave my country because of the political unrest that prevailed there. Five years later, when I was twenty-six, I was introduced to The Church of Jesus Christ of Latter-day Saints. I loved the feeling of peace that I experienced there. I was baptized in the Church in November of 1989.

As the holiday season drew nearer that year, we started singing Christmas hymns at Church. As I sang them, a special feeling overwhelmed me. For the first time in my life, I knew what the true spirit of Christmas was. I felt so much reverence for the birth of our Savior. It reminded me of the reverence I would feel when as a child I would gently lay Baby Jesus in our Nativity set on Christmas Eve. Jesus Christ was born in a humble place to fulfill His divine mission, to obey the will of His Father, and to show us the way back to Him. His birth marks the beginning of a new era for humanity. He came to save us, to teach us, to inspire us, to love us, and to enable us so that we can break the bonds of sin and death and be sanctified and cleansed through His Atonement and through our obedience to His gospel. He said: "I am the way, the truth and the life: no man cometh unto the Father, but by me" (John 14:6).

It was more than forty years after that earthquake in Managua that one day I received a revelation as I was doing dishes in the kitchen of my home in Orem, Utah. It was Easter time, a time when we ponder the Resurrection of the Lord. I was reflecting about what that magnificent gift means to us. I started thinking about my brother Noelito. At that moment, something clicked in my mind. I remembered that daydream in which I had imagined him coming to me after he was dead. All those years, I never told anybody about my daydream, because I always thought that it was silly, that it was just my imagination. But that day in the kitchen, I realized that it had really been the Light of Christ that had come to me as a little girl who needed comfort in that moment of her life.

Through the Lord's immense love and power, I had received a witness that my brother's spirit is not dead; he is alive. Noelito is just somewhere else, in another state, still progressing in his eternal existence. He is "departed from the mortal life, firm in the hope of a glorious resurrection" (D&C 138:14). He is waiting for that magnificent moment in which we will all be resurrected, be reunited as a family, be able to have joy in ways we cannot imagine, and have the opportunity to progress and learn even more, in the presence of our heavenly parents and our Lord Jesus Christ.

That revelation was a moment of glory, joy, and gratitude for me. How merciful the Lord was with me, that He allowed me to see the truth of the Resurrection in my life when I had needed it. Thanks to Him and to the fact that He was resurrected, we will all be resurrected after we die. At that moment, our "soul shall be restored to the body . . . [and] all things shall be restored to their proper and perfect frame" (Alma 40:23). We will be in a different state in our path through our eternal existence.

The birth of Christ, our Savior, brought His light to the world, a light that brings knowledge, comfort, healing, peace, power, and revelation to all who seek Him. Because of His Resurrection, "the grave [has] no victory, and the sting of death can be swallowed up in Christ. He is the light and the life of the world; yea, a light that is endless, that can never be darkened; yea, and also a life which is endless, that there can be no more death" (Mosiah 16:8–9). As we turn to our Savior, remember Him in all of our thoughts and actions, and strive to follow His commandments, His light can guide us, His love can comfort us, and His power can enable us to do what we cannot do by ourselves.

WE CAN REACH FOR THE SAVIOR
WHEN WE TRUST THAT HIS BIRTH, LIFE,
AND RESURRECTION OFFERED ALL OF
US THE GIFT OF ETERNAL LIFE.

THE BODY OF CHRIST

I separated from my first husband in 1989 because of his addiction to alcohol and drugs. This was a difficult decision for me to make because we had a three-year-old boy at the time, but I felt that it was the right thing to do. Nevertheless, I felt despair, fear, and uncertainty about the future.

About three weeks after that final separation, my mother went to visit her sister, who lived a few blocks away from us in San Francisco. My aunt, her husband, and some of their children belonged to The Church of Jesus Christ of Latter-day Saints. They had been members for a few years and had invited us to come and attend that church many times. At that point in my life, I believed in God but did not know how much I needed to get closer to Him, and I had not accepted their invitations.

During my mother's visit to my aunt that day, a senior missionary couple, Elder Leland Bangerter and Sister Valois Bangerter, came to my aunt's apartment and had a chat with my mother. They showed her a video and invited her to church the next day. When I got home from work that evening, my mother told me about her conversation with the missionaries and their invitation to go to church. Because of all the hardship that I had just gone through, this time I was ready to accept the invitation.

The next day was a Sunday, and it was October 15, 1989. We drove to my aunt's apartment so we could all drive together to church. The missionaries were happy to see us, and we followed them to the meetinghouse in San Bruno, a city south of San Francisco.

That was the day when my life changed for good. I did not know what to expect, but the moment that I stepped into that building, I had this wonderful feeling that I was in a sacred place. There were a lot of people, and everyone seemed happy.

It was a stake conference, where several congregational units met, and a few people gave spiritual messages. Since it was in English and I was not familiar with some of the terms, I did not understand everything. For example, they mentioned the word "gospel" several times. I was not sure what that meant, but I could tell that it was a good thing. The Light of Christ spoke to my soul in a way that transcended language, time, and space. It was a different feeling from what I had ever felt before.

Every message seemed to be given directly to me. One of the

speakers gave a message about Hurricane Hugo. He told the story of a family in a Caribbean island whose house started flooding and they kept going to the higher levels of their home until they ended up on the roof, from where they were rescued. He said that those people were looking for a safer place so they could be protected, and that the gospel was like that because it helps us get closer to our Heavenly Father and our Savior Jesus Christ. It provides a safe place where we can be protected. As I heard that, I felt the desire to learn more about that "gospel."

At that point in my life, I needed to find peace and solace for my soul. I needed to find a place where I could help my son become a good man. Sitting in that meeting, I knew I had found a haven for me and my son. I was filled with hope as I listened to the speakers.

Later on, I learned that Elder Quentin L. Cook was the stake president at that stake conference. Years later, he became an Apostle of the Lord, and now our paths in the service of God have once again crossed. It is wonderful to reflect on the influence that our sincere efforts to serve the Lord can make on others. Everyone involved in that stake conference contributed to inviting the Spirit, which helped me turn to my Heavenly Father and my Savior so They could extend Their mercy to me.

After the meeting ended, there was so much excitement around me. Everyone was smiling and they were so cheerful. As we were leaving the building, I approached the missionaries and asked them, "Could you please come to our home? Could you please teach us more?"

They joyfully replied, "Of course! We would be happy to do that!"

We agreed on meeting the following Tuesday at 8:00 p.m., and I was looking forward to that evening. I had the feeling that my life was going to take a significant turn.

The day came. It was Tuesday, around 5:00 p.m. I was at work with my son Xavier and Annie, the girl I nannied. We were at her house and the children were playing in Annie's room. I was sitting on the floor watching them play. Suddenly, the ground started shaking. It was the 6.9-magnitude Loma Prieta earthquake that rocked the San Francisco Bay Area. I embraced the children and just waited. The trembling lasted for what seemed a long time.

Annie's parents came home as soon as they could, and then I drove home. I prepared myself to be driving through chaos. Many streetlights were down. However, the traffic was flowing in an orderly manner. In some busy corners, there were civilians helping to direct the traffic. If there was no one doing that, drivers would stop at every corner and follow the four-stop rule. I was impressed to see how the goodness of people surfaces when tragedy strikes.

Getting home took much longer than normal. There was rubble on some streets, and damage could be seen on the walls of some buildings. As soon as I got home, I called the missionaries to tell them that we should probably postpone our meeting. They agreed because there was no electricity in some neighborhoods and the city looked darker than usual.

My mother, my sister Sandra, my brother Henry, my son Xavier, and I were finally able to meet with the missionaries a couple of days after the earthquake. Their messages were so simple, and yet profound. They taught me that God is close to us—that we can talk to Him and He listens, that we have a Savior and Redeemer, and because of Him we can overcome the struggles of mortality and have the hope of eternal life. They said that we can live with our families forever. As the missionaries taught us, we felt something different in our home. They were full of joy, and I could tell how much they loved each other. Their happiness was contagious, and I had a deep desire to feel the way these missionaries did.

They came to our home several times over the following three weeks. During one of our meetings, they asked each of us if we would like to be baptized. I thought for a few seconds, and then said, "Yes!" My mother and my brother also agreed. The missionaries got excited, and we decided on a date for our baptism. We chose Sunday, November 5, as the day when we would enter the waters of baptism.

The day arrived. Sacrament service at church was different that day. People from the congregation got up to express their feelings and testify about the gospel of Jesus Christ and the Church, which I later learned was called fast and testimony meeting. My mother also got up and told everyone how she was feeling. She said that as she was sitting there, listening to everyone, she asked in her heart, "God, is this church really true?" Right after that, she felt warmth inside of her and knew for certain that it was true.

We went back to the San Bruno meetinghouse that evening so we could get baptized. Many members of the branch showed up. Elder Bangerter baptized the three of us and then he conferred the gift of the Holy Ghost to us. Receiving the gift of the Holy Ghost and knowing that I could have that gift with me if I was faithful made me feel complete and whole—I finally felt a sense of belonging. I loved the feeling that I had. I felt clean! I truly believed that if I had a sincere desire to have faith and to make changes in my life, the sacrifice that Jesus Christ made for all of us could help me to "be purified even as he is pure" (Moroni 7:48) and to face life in a better way, "armed with righteousness and with the power of God in great glory" (1 Nephi 14:14).

Everyone at church seemed to be happy about our decision to get baptized. They made us feel welcomed, that we were at home, and that we had found a new family among them.

Life continued, but it was not the same. I felt different, and I could see that something was happening inside me. Thanks to the baptismal covenant I had made and kept with my Savior, I was starting to feel peace and hope for the future. My heart "changed through faith on his name" (Mosiah 5:7).

A few days after our baptism, something magnificent happened. The Berlin Wall came down. People in Germany were being reunited with relatives that they had not seen in a long time.

The entire world was watching in awe as a symbol of captivity, injustice, and sorrow collapsed. For me, these events were particularly significant because they were happening while crucial events were occurring in my life. I looked at them as a sign of changes and of a better future for me and my son.

Being a member of The Church of Jesus Christ of Latter-day Saints was such an enormous blessing in every way. Sunday was the highlight of the week for me. Every message that I heard at sacrament meeting, every class that I attended, and every conversation that I had with members of the Church felt to me like a never-ending stream of knowledge, faith, and strength coming to me. Every concept was explained in such a way that helped me see God, the world, and myself differently.

Having the opportunity to take the sacrament each week was a great blessing. I loved the feeling of reverence that I felt during that time. The words of the sacrament prayers are so beautiful. We tell our Heavenly Father that we are willing to take upon us the name of His Son, to always remember Him, and to keep His commandments. In return, we receive the promise that we may always have His Spirit to be with us (see D&C 20:77–79). I believe in the words of King Benjamin when he spoke about the "blessed and happy state of those that keep the commandments of God. For behold, they are blessed in all things, both temporal and spiritual; and if they hold out faithful to the end they are received into heaven, that thereby they may dwell with God in a state of never-ending happiness" (Mosiah 2:41). I am so grateful to my Heavenly Father and my Lord Jesus Christ for allowing me to receive all of those blessings at that time in my life. I found something that I did not know I was missing. I hope and pray that I will never lose that feeling of amazement.

People come to the Church from all different circumstances—for some, a missionary knocks on their door; some are born into families who are already members; some ask a certain friend or neighbor what it is that makes that person different and happy. However, as we come to join with the Saints, we each must make the choice to take the name of Christ upon us and live according to the baptismal covenant we have made.

Each of us can be the means through which others feel the love of God in their life. Through our righteousness, our sincere desire to follow the commandments, and our constant effort to minister to others in simple ways, people can perceive God's image in our countenance, and they can have the desire to follow Him. "And the Lord doth work by means to bring about his great and eternal purposes" (Alma 37:7).

WE CAN REACH FOR THE SAVIOR BY
TAKING HIS NAME UPON US AS WE
MAKE SACRED BAPTISMAL COVENANTS
AND JOIN WITH HIS CHURCH.

SERVING IN THE CHURCH
AND RELIEF SOCIETY

As soon as I was called as the Second Counselor in the Relief Society General Presidency in April 2017, this question came pounding in my mind: "What is Relief Society?"

Reading about the history of Relief Society has given me a better perspective of the purpose of this divine organization. I have marveled at the knowledge that Relief Society is "a restoration of an ancient pattern"[1] and "that the same organization existed in the church anciently."[2] As I have studied the New Testament, I have seen many examples of "female disciples" who "journeyed with Jesus and His Twelve Apostles [and gave] of their substance to assist in His ministry." I have also learned that "after His death and Resurrection, women continued to be faithful disciples. They met and prayed together with the Apostles. They provided their homes as gathering places for Church members [and] valiantly participated in the work of saving souls, temporally and spiritually."[3] I have read about Martha and her sister Mary, about Mary Magdalene, Joanna, Susanna, Tabitha, Priscilla, and many others who were "converted unto the Lord" (3 Nephi 28:23) and who worked tirelessly to bring His gospel to others.

I have rejoiced at the thought that as part of the Restoration during this "dispensation of the fulness of times" (D&C 128:18), the Relief Society was organized by the Prophet Joseph Smith through priesthood keys and "after the pattern of the priesthood"[4] so women could "do something extraordinary."[5]

Regarding Relief Society, President Joseph F. Smith said, "This organization is divinely made, divinely authorized, divinely instituted, divinely ordained of God to minister for the salvation of the souls of women and of men."[6]

As I continued reading and learning, a second question came to my mind: "What has Relief Society been for me?"

My thoughts went back to the time when I was living in San Francisco, California, being taught by the missionaries, Elder and Sister Bangerter. I immediately felt a connection with that sweet, enthusiastic, and faithful sister who, together with her husband, was preaching the gospel in that little corner of the world that was our home. From them, I learned about my Heavenly Father and His "great plan of salvation" (Alma 42:5) and about the redeeming Atonement of Jesus Christ. I learned about repentance, the covenant of baptism, and the promise of forgiveness and eternal life. I learned about the Prophet Joseph Smith and his role in the Restoration; about the commandments and the promised blessings that we can receive if we make a sincere effort to obey them, among many other profound and yet simple concepts.

The soothing relationship that I have had with that devoted sister missionary was only the first of countless significant relationships and eternal bonds that I have been able to establish over the years with many faithful daughters of our glorious Mother Eve (see D&C 138:39).

After I joined The Church of Jesus Christ of Latter-day Saints, the members of a small Spanish-speaking branch in San Francisco embraced me with their love. All of a sudden, I had friends, teachers, leaders, counselors, and role models of all ages, male and female, and through their words and actions I could feel the Holy Ghost testifying of the truth of the restored gospel of Jesus Christ in my heart.

As I listened and watched all of them, a whole new realm of knowledge, faith, testimony, and love came to my life. I still vividly remember the feelings of amazement that I had at every sacrament meeting, every Gospel Doctrine class, and every Relief Society meeting. It was a never-ending flow of tender mercies of the Lord that came to me through the faithful members of that small branch, who taught me so much with their example and the joyful way they lived the gospel.

A few weeks after I was baptized, my visiting teachers came to my home, and they brought a warm feeling of belonging and love to my heart. I then learned that I could also do the same thing they were doing, so I could bring that same warm feeling to other sisters.

Shortly after, I learned that as an adult female member of the Church, I belonged to Relief Society. I also learned that in our Church we are not just passive observers and recipients of information and counsel, but we can be active contributors and participants. I discovered that the members of our Church are blessed with the opportunity to have callings. Sure enough, members of the branch presidency approached me with an opportunity to serve, and then with another, and another.

When my first assignment to give a talk in sacrament meeting came from the branch president, a sweet and wise sister patiently guided me through the process of preparing a talk. She taught me how to find passages of scripture that were related to the assigned topic and gently guided me so I could receive my own revelation through promptings from the Holy Ghost.

As I served in those first callings and assignments, and all the ones that came after, there have always been loving sisters surrounding me and teaching me by example how faithful female disciples of the Lord Jesus Christ serve and love. As I look back, I can see that each of them has left a lasting imprint in my life. They taught me how to transition from being a recent convert to becoming "converted unto the Lord" (4 Nephi 1:2). They literally took my hand and showed me the way.

To His servants, the Lord has promised: "I will go before your face. I will be on your right hand and on your left, and my Spirit shall be in your hearts, and mine angels round about you, to bear you up" (D&C 84:88). Through my life, before and after I joined the Church, I have felt those angels around me, both from the other side of the veil and from this side.

Many of those angels have come to me wearing a white shirt and a tie, ministering to my spiritual needs and using priesthood keys and offices to bring light and guidance to my life, but also wearing working clothes and with a tool in their hand to bring comfort and help when I have needed them. Many other angels have come to me wearing a skirt, taking me by the hand, and showing me how to be a female disciple of Jesus Christ, but also wearing everyday clothes to support me and to allow me to cry on their shoulder when I needed that.

So, what has Relief Society meant for me? It has meant a never-ending wealth of assistance from heaven and from earth that has helped me begin to prepare for the blessings of eternal life.

For me, Relief Society has been the relationships that I have cultivated with faithful women, the love that I have felt from and for other sisters as we have worked together on "the errand of angels,"[7] and the truths that I have learned as I have tried to fulfill my purpose and mission, in spirit and deed,[8] as a woman in Zion.

Those women and the fruits of their labors have been a source of guidance that has helped me understand my role as a daughter of God, a wife, and a mother. They have inspired me as I have struggled to keep a balance between my responsibilities with God, myself, my family, my home, my callings, and my job. They have shown me how to set priorities in my life so I can find time for the daily sacred habits that give me the spiritual strength I need when the road ahead looks steep.

As we face the world during these latter days and as we strive to keep the covenants that we have made with God so we can fulfill "the measure of [our] creation" (D&C 88:19), Relief Society can be a haven for us women. As President Boyd K. Packer has promised: "This great circle of sisters will be a protection for each of you and for your families. The Relief Society might be likened to a refuge—the place of safety and protection—the sanctuary of ancient times. You will be safe within it. It encircles each sister like a protecting wall."[9]

The prophet President Thomas S. Monson said: "You, my beloved sisters, know who you are and what God expects you to become. Your challenge is to bring all for whom you are responsible to a knowledge of this truth. The Relief Society of this, the Lord's Church, can be the means to achieve such a goal."[10]

Jean B. Bingham, General Relief Society President, taught: "Although each woman is unique, there are feelings and divine gifts and experiences that we have in common which bind us together. We are daughters of our heavenly parents, who love us and want us to become like Them. We are full partners with the priesthood in the work of salvation—the saving of the souls of men and women—which is the focus of all our efforts. As sisters and brothers, we were given and accepted responsibilities in the premortal world for building the Kingdom of God on the earth. . . .

[We] may not realize it yet, but Relief Society can help [us] accomplish extraordinary things."[11]

I have been approached by sisters who have sheepishly apologized to me. They think they are not active members of Relief Society because they are serving in Primary or Young Women. I give a hug to those sisters and tell them that they are among the most active members of Relief Society because they are fulfilling their calling and helping our precious children and youth strengthen their faith in Heavenly Father and our Savior Jesus Christ. In my own experience, some of my greatest spiritual lessons as a Relief Society sister came when I was working with the youth.

For example, years ago, when I was a Young Women leader, my responsibilities included being over Young Women camp. My first two times as a camp leader were extremely exhausting for me. Both times, by the end of the first day at camp, I was so stressed that it was hard for me to fall asleep. Exhaustion would make the second day even harder than the first one. By the time camp was over, I did not have much energy left and I had missed opportunities to feel true joy during the week.

Before I left for camp the third year, I worried that I would once again be so physically drained that I would not be able to contribute to an atmosphere that would allow the young women and us leaders to have a spiritual experience at camp.

So before camp week that year, I expressed my concerns to my husband and asked him to give me a priesthood blessing so I could receive divine guidance and inspiration. He blessed me, among other things, with the ability to discern what was more important during camp, to focus there, and to let secondary things go. He also said, "Let the Holy Ghost guide you." Those words pierced my heart and gave me the direction I needed so desperately.

I left for camp, and as the days went by, I strived to remember to focus on what was more important by truly letting the Holy Ghost guide me, hour after hour, day after day.

On the last day at camp, as I was walking uphill to my car, carrying a relatively heavy bag on my shoulder, I realized that I was not tired. I thought to myself, *This is the last day of camp, and I'm not exhausted. What happened?* I then realized that even though I had had a busy and demanding week, my perspective on the everyday details had been totally different from previous years, and that had made a big difference.

At that moment, I remembered the Lord's invitation and promise: "Come unto me, all ye that labour and are heavy laden, and I will give you rest. Take my yoke upon you, and learn of me; for I am meek and lowly in heart: and ye shall find rest unto your souls. For my yoke is easy, and my burden is light" (Matthew 11:28–30).

As I looked back, I could remember the little things that I had done differently that week. First, I did not feel like the whole camp experience depended on me. While taking responsibility for the things I had to do, I allowed others to make choices and do their part. I finally let the young women be the leaders, as it is supposed to be. Second, I made sure to eat well and drink plenty of water. I made small adjustments in my routine so I could have enough sleep, and that was a big help. Most importantly, I let the Lord guide me through the Holy Ghost so I could discern where I needed to invest my energy and efforts and what could be done either by someone else, at another time, or not at all.

I learned from that experience that my service as a leader—in Primary, in Young Women, in Relief Society, in my home, or anywhere else—is not about me. It is all about the Lord and the people I serve. I learned that what matters the most is what I am becoming as I allow the Lord to refine me. I learned that even though I need to make my best effort, I cannot do it all myself and I must depend on Jesus Christ's divine grace. I learned that I need to be wise in managing my energy, my sanity, and my spirituality, so I can give the Lord my best offering in helping Him to do His work. And He certainly did. He changed me, He tutored me, He guided me, and He allowed me to feel joy in that demanding environment that I had not felt before. I learned that "I can do all things through Christ which strengtheneth me" (Philippians 4:13). I have tried to carry those lessons with me and have found that they can strengthen my efforts no matter where I am asked to serve.

Relief Society is not a room in a meetinghouse, it is not an hour meeting on a Sunday, and it is not an activity for women in the Church. Relief Society is the women of the Church; it is us, each of us, all of us. It is the greatest organization of women in the world, not only because of the millions of women who belong to it, but mainly because of its purpose, which is for covenant women to accomplish the work of salvation and exaltation in an organized way.

Sharon Eubank, First Counselor in the General Relief Society Presidency, said, "Relief Society . . . is organized under priesthood keys for women to have a place to grow, progress, build their faith, talk about the reality of family life, and mourn with each other for all the . . . things that happen to us when we are mortals. We cannot give in to those voices who say it's just like a sewing circle or a book club for people who have the same interests and backgrounds. No, Relief Society has a work to do on the earth. When you belong to Relief Society, you are part of that work. The Lord has a stewardship for His daughters in the work of salvation, and only we can do it. It can only be done by women who are truly converted unto the Lord."[12]

Over the years, I have learned that there are divine reasons why we, as men and women, are organized in priesthood quorums and Relief Societies in The Church of Jesus Christ of Latter-day Saints. In the kingdom of God, we have work to do—as individuals, as families, and as priesthood quorums and Relief Societies.

Sister Julie B. Beck, former General Relief Society President explained:

"A priesthood quorum is a group of men . . . who are to perform a special labor. . . .

". . . 'The Relief Society is the Lord's organization for women'[13] . . . The word *society* has a meaning nearly identical to that of *quorum*. It connotes 'an enduring and cooperating . . . group' distinguished by its common aims and beliefs."

She went on to illustrate "five important reasons why we are organized into quorums and Relief Societies." First, "to organize us under the priesthood and after the pattern of the priesthood." Second, "to focus Heavenly Father's sons and daughters on the work of salvation and to engage them in it." Third, "to help bishops wisely manage the Lord's storehouse." Fourth, "to provide a defense and a refuge for Heavenly Father's children and their families in the latter days." And fifth, "to strengthen and support us in our family roles and responsibilities as sons and daughters of God."[14]

Why does it matter that each of us connects ourselves with our quorum or Relief Society? I testify that doing so helps us be part of the most important work there is. President Russell M. Nelson has said, "Our Savior and Redeemer, Jesus Christ, will perform some of His mightiest works between now and when He comes again."[15] As Jesus Christ's disciples we need to be active participants in His works.

The Lord Himself has said: "Behold, *I will hasten my work in its time.* And I give unto you, who are the first laborers in this last kingdom, a commandment that you assemble yourselves together, and organize yourselves, and prepare yourselves, and sanctify yourselves; yea, purify your hearts, and cleanse your hands and your feet before me, that I may make you clean" (D&C 88:73–74; emphasis added).

President Nelson has invited us to gather Israel on both sides of the veil. If we are to accomplish "*the greatest* challenge, *the greatest* cause, and *the greatest* work on earth today,"[16] we need to labor together—at the individual level; at the family level; as members of the divinely organized priesthood quorums and Relief Societies;

interdependently as members of our wards, stakes, and the Church as a whole; and under the direction of priesthood keys.

"In ecclesiastical callings, temple ordinances, family relationships, and quiet, individual ministry, Latter-day Saint women and men go forward with priesthood power and authority. This interdependence of men and women in accomplishing God's work through His power is central to the gospel of Jesus Christ restored through the Prophet Joseph Smith"[17] and will help prepare the world for the Savior's Second Coming.

Sheri L. Dew, former Second Counselor in the Relief Society General Presidency, said to the women of the Church, "We are here to influence the world rather than to be influenced by the world. If we could unleash the full influence of covenant-keeping women, the kingdom of God would change overnight."[18] I also believe that the female disciples of Jesus Christ can and do influence the world and that there is still much potential inside us that could still do more good as we keep our covenants and as we participate in preparing the earth for the glorious return of Jesus Christ.

WE CAN REACH FOR THE SAVIOR WHEN
WE LABOR TOGETHER AS WOMEN IN ZION,
INTERDEPENDENTLY WITH MEN, TO SHARE
THE JOY OF THE GOSPEL WITH OTHERS.

NOTES

1. *Daughters in My Kingdom: The History and Work of Relief Society* (2011), 3.
2. Eliza R. Snow, in *Daughters in My Kingdom*, 7.
3. *Daughters in My Kingdom*, 3.
4. Joseph Smith, in *Daughters in My Kingdom*, 12.
5. Emma Smith, in *Daughters in My Kingdom*, 14.
6. *Teachings of Presidents of the Church: Joseph F. Smith* (1998), 184.
7. "As Sisters in Zion," *Hymns*, no. 309.
8. See "As Sisters in Zion," *Hymns*, no. 309.
9. Boyd K. Packer, in *Daughters in My Kingdom*, 86.
10. Thomas S. Monson, "If Ye Are Prepared Ye Shall Not Fear," *Ensign*, Nov. 2004, 115.
11. Jean B. Bingham, "How Vast is Our Purpose," Brigham Young University Women's Conference address, May 2017.
12. Sharon Eubank, "Eyes to See, Discipline to Create, Glue to Bind—Converted unto the Lord," Brigham Young University Women's Conference address, May 2017.
13. *Teachings of Presidents of the Church: Spencer W. Kimball* (2006), 217.
14. Julie B. Beck, "Why We Are Organized into Quorums and Relief Societies" (Brigham Young University devotional, Jan. 12, 2012), speeches.byu.edu.
15. Russell M. Nelson, "Revelation for the Church, Revelation for Our Lives," *Ensign*, May 2018, 96.
16. Russell M. Nelson, "Hope of Israel" (worldwide youth devotional, June 3, 2018), HopeofIsrael.ChurchofJesusChrist.org.
17. "Joseph Smith's Teachings about Priesthood, Temple, Women," Gospel Topics, topics.ChurchofJesusChrist.org.
18. Sheri Dew, "Awake, Arise, and Come Unto Christ," Brigham Young University Women's Conference address, May 2008.

A GIFT OF GOD'S PRIESTHOOD POWER

President Russell M. Nelson has taught: "Every woman and every man who makes covenants with God and keeps those covenants, and who participates worthily in priesthood ordinances, has direct access to the power of God. Those who are endowed in the house of the Lord receive a gift of God's priesthood power by virtue of their covenant, along with a gift of knowledge to know how to draw upon that power." And then, speaking to the women of the Church, he said, "Sisters, you have the right to draw liberally upon the Savior's power to help your family and others you love. . . . As your understanding increases and as you exercise faith in the Lord and His priesthood power, your ability to draw upon this spiritual treasure that the Lord has made available will increase."[1]

I have seen many examples of women and men receiving that gift of God's priesthood power in their life. I will mention two. The first one is a widow I met in the Democratic Republic of the Congo. Kinshasa is a vibrant city, but there is a lot of poverty. To get to this sister's house, you leave the main road and walk through a little alley between homes. Her house is tiny. She has four girls. She tried to get support from her family when her husband died, but they were poor themselves and could not help her. She had to go out and do it by herself. Her daughters could not attend school because she could not afford the uniforms. She felt bad that they all could not go to school. Then, she heard about a school run by Latter-day Saint service missionaries and started sending her daughters there.

This family eventually joined the Church, but the woman still was not self-reliant. The ward council suggested she might start a business. The Kinshasa Temple was under construction at that time, so she began a little business selling food to the workers building the temple. That made such a difference in her life. She had just a tiny refrigerator and a few pots. She went to the temple construction site every day to sell food. Her business grew enough that she made sufficient money to support her girls in school. Eventually, her oldest daughter attended college.

It caught my attention when I visited her that she had a long mirror in the corner of her living room. She had that mirror, some plastic chairs, a table, and a small bookcase. When I saw the mirror, I knew she had bought it for her daughters so they could see themselves, how beautiful they are, and who they could become. Our covenants are like a mirror. They help us see ourselves, but also our future; where we are now, and where the Lord wants us to go. Just imagine what will happen to this woman and all the blessings that will come to her. The covenants she made with God changed everything about her life. The baptismal covenant and the gift of the Holy Ghost gave her power to pull her family together. Temporally and spiritually, she found power when she had none. Now that the Kinshasa Temple has been dedicated, she has the opportunity to be endowed with greater "power from on high" (D&C 95:8).

The second story is about a couple from Argentina living in Orem, Utah. The wife was baptized but her husband was not. He was a good man and attended church with her for many years. People thought he was already a member. Finally, after some time, he was baptized too. My husband, Carlos, and I could not go to the baptismal service, but we saw the man the next day. Carlos asked me with surprise, "Did you see him? He looks so different! What happened to him?" He was a different person. He just shined. Even though he had been going to church, when he finally made his own baptismal covenant, priesthood power began to operate in his life. Eventually, this couple received their endowment and were sealed to each other before going back to Argentina. We heard a year later that he had been called as a bishop. His life and his growth were accelerated dramatically when he made covenants, but it took patience and time.

So, how do we receive priesthood power? Just like the individuals in these two stories, *every woman and man receives priesthood power as she or he participates in priesthood ordinances and keeps the related covenants.* These include the covenants made at baptism and in the temple.[2] We learn in the Doctrine and Covenants that access to priesthood power also requires personal righteousness, "gentleness, meekness, and love unfeigned" (D&C 121:41). Each woman can draw upon priesthood power according to her covenants and her personal righteousness. No one can take it from her, but no one can give priesthood power to her outside of the covenants and her individual striving to live true to those covenants.

When we keep the commandments, there are specific blessings and promises given by the Lord. Here are a few examples from the scriptures:

- When we pay tithing, the Lord says, "I will . . . open you the windows of heaven . . . and pour you out a blessing, that there shall not be room enough to receive it" (Malachi 3:10).
- When we keep the Word of Wisdom, we "shall find wisdom and great treasures of knowledge" (see D&C 89:18–21).
- When we participate actively in the Church and minister to others, "the angels cannot be restrained from being [our] associates."[3]
- And when we keep our baptismal and temple covenants, "the doctrine of the priesthood shall distill upon [our] soul as the dews from heaven" (D&C 121:45–46).

I always feel sad when I hear a woman say, "I don't have the priesthood in my home." She generally means there is no one holding a priesthood office living in her home. Be assured that a single woman or a woman whose husband does not hold a priesthood office does not need to feel she is cut off from priesthood power and blessings. These sisters can draw upon priesthood power through their covenants, and the faithfulness with which they keep those covenants can bless every member of their household. And while they will call on brothers who hold a Melchizedek Priesthood office for blessings of health or comfort, they are nevertheless themselves a source of priesthood power for their own homes.

President M. Russell Ballard said this: "All men and all women have access to this power for help in their lives. All who have made sacred covenants with the Lord and who honor those covenants are eligible to receive personal revelation, to be blessed by the ministering of angels, to commune with God, to receive the fulness of the gospel, and, ultimately, to become heirs alongside Jesus Christ of all our Father has."[4]

Some confusion arises because there is a difference between priesthood *power* and priesthood *authority.*

Priesthood *power* is God's power in the lives of men and women who keep their covenants. Priesthood *authority* is the permission or license to perform specific priesthood duties and comes from ordination to priesthood office and from being set apart for callings in the Church.[5]

Priesthood authority is conferred by the laying on of hands

under the direction of those who have priesthood keys. Women receive this authority in the form of a calling. Men receive this authority in the form of a calling or an office in the priesthood. President Dallin H. Oaks made that clear when he said, "Whoever functions in an office or calling received from one who holds priesthood keys exercises priesthood authority in performing her or his assigned duties."[6]

A man or woman with priesthood *authority* will have no priesthood *power* if he or she is unworthy or seeks to exercise control, dominion, or compulsion upon others in any degree of unrighteousness.[7]

Priesthood power is not the same as worldly power. The worldly view of power is that "I can do whatever I want, I can tell you what to do, I am in charge and you have to obey." I like how one insightful sister expressed this thought: "In the world, having power generally [involves] amassing money, goods, knowledge, and authority, and using those things to gain influence, approval, status, or control over other people. By contrast, in the kingdom of God, the purpose of having power, resources, knowledge, and authority is to pass them on, using them to empower others to get power of their own, become more like God, and enter His presence."[8]

As Linda K. Burton, former Relief Society General President expressed it, "Righteousness is the qualifier for each of us to invite priesthood power into our lives."[9]

I invite each of us to pay close attention to the words expressed in every priesthood ordinance. Listen for every time the word "priesthood" is spoken in the temple. How does that apply to you? How does it bless you?

I know that we receive power through making and keeping covenants, and our personal righteousness, and I know that we can use that power to bless our lives and the lives of others.

WE CAN REACH FOR THE SAVIOR WHEN WE KEEP OUR COVENANTS IN RIGHTEOUSNESS AND DRAW UPON GOD'S PRIESTHOOD POWER.

NOTES

1. Russell M. Nelson, "Spiritual Treasures," *Ensign*, Nov. 2019, 77–79.
2. See M. Russell Ballard, "Let Us Think Straight," Brigham Young University Education Week devotional, Aug. 20, 2013; see also Doctrine and Covenants 84:20.
3. History of the Church, 4:604–5; from a discourse given by Joseph Smith on Apr. 28, 1842, in Nauvoo, Illinois; reported by Eliza R. Snow.
4. M. Russell Ballard, "Men and Women and Priesthood Power," *Ensign*, Sept. 2014, 32.
5. See Dallin H. Oaks, "The Keys and Authority of the Priesthood," *Ensign*, May 2014, 49–52.
6. Oaks, "The Keys and Authority of the Priesthood."
7. See Doctrine and Covenants 121:34–45.
8. Wendy Ulrich, *Live Up to Our Privileges* (Salt Lake City: Deseret Book, 2019), 7.
9. Linda K. Burton, "Priesthood: 'A Sacred Trust to Be Used for the Benefit of Men, Women, and Children,'" Brigham Young University Women's Conference address, May 3, 2013.

WITH ONE ACCORD

One of the most remarkable creatures on earth is the monarch butterfly. On a trip to Mexico to spend Christmas with my husband's family, we visited a majestic forest that is a butterfly sanctuary, where millions of monarch butterflies spend the winter. It was fascinating to see such an impressive sight and for us to reflect on the example of unity and obedience to divine laws that God's creations demonstrate (see Abraham 4:7, 9–12, 15, 18, 21, 24–25; 3:26).

Monarch butterflies are master navigators. They use the sun's position to find the direction they need to go. Every spring, they travel thousands of miles from Mexico to Canada, and every fall, they return to the same sacred fir forests in Mexico.[1] They do this year after year, one tiny wing flap at a time. Even though they travel alone during the day, they cluster together at night on trees, to protect themselves from the cold and from predators.[2] When they are together, it looks like they are dancing to music that we cannot hear; as if they see something that we cannot see and know something that we do not know. They have a definite purpose.

A group of butterflies is called a kaleidoscope.[3] Isn't that a beautiful image? Each butterfly in a kaleidoscope is unique and different, yet these seemingly fragile creatures have been designed by a loving Creator with the ability to survive, travel, multiply, and disseminate life, as they go from one flower to the next, spreading pollen. Although each butterfly is different, they work together to make the world a more beautiful and fruitful place.

Like the monarch butterflies, we are on a journey back to our heavenly home where we will reunite with our heavenly parents.[4] Like the butterflies, we have been given divine attributes that allow us to navigate through life, in order to fill "the measure of [our] creation" (D&C 88:19). Like them, if we knit our hearts together, the Lord will protect us "as a hen [gathers] her chickens under her wings" (3 Nephi 10:4) and will make us into a beautiful kaleidoscope.

We are all on this journey together. To reach our sublime destiny, we need each other, and we need to be unified. The Lord has commanded us, "Be one; and if ye are not one ye are not mine" (D&C 38:27).

Jesus Christ is the ultimate example of unity with His Father.

They are one in purpose, in love, and in works, with "the will of the Son being swallowed up in the will of the Father" (Mosiah 15:7).

How can we follow the Lord's perfect example of unity with His Father and be more unified with Them and with each other?

An inspiring pattern is found in Acts 1:14. We read: "[The men] all continued *with one accord* in prayer and supplication with the women" (emphasis added).

I think it is significant that the phrase "with one accord" appears several times in the book of Acts,[5] where we read about what Jesus Christ's followers did immediately after He ascended to heaven as a resurrected being, as well as the blessings they received because of their efforts. It is also significant that we find a similar pattern among the faithful of the American continent at the time the Lord visited and ministered to them. "With one accord" means in agreement, in unity, and all together.

Some of the things that the faithful Saints did in unity in both places were that they testified of Jesus Christ, studied the word of God, and ministered to each other with love.[6]

The Lord's followers were one in purpose, in love, and in works. They knew who they were, they knew what they had to do, and they did it with love for God and for each other. They were part of a magnificent kaleidoscope moving forward with one accord.

Some of the blessings they received were that they were filled with the Holy Ghost, miracles took place among them, the Church grew, there was no contention among the people, and the Lord blessed them in all things.[7]

We can suppose that the reason why they were so united is that they knew the Lord personally. They had been close to Him, and they had been witnesses of His divine mission, of the miracles that He performed, of His Crucifixion, and of His Resurrection. They saw and touched the marks in His hands and feet. They knew with certainty that He was the promised Messiah, the Redeemer of the world. They knew that "He is the source of all healing, peace, and eternal progress."[8]

Even though we may not have seen our Savior with our physical eyes, we can know that He lives. As we draw closer to Him, as we seek to receive a personal witness through the Holy Ghost of His divine mission, we will have a better understanding of our purpose; the love of God will dwell in our hearts (see 4 Nephi 1:15); we will have the determination to be one in the kaleidoscopes of our families, wards, and communities; and we will minister to each other "in newer, better ways."[9]

Miracles happen when the children of God work together guided by the Spirit to reach out to others in need.

After that terrifying night of the earthquake in 1972, when my family lost everything, including my brother, we received so much help from so many people. Our relatives, our neighbors, our friends, and even total strangers were kind to us. I do not remember ever being hungry or cold. I always had food and a place to sleep.

I later heard that the morning after the earthquake, as my

parents were waiting for the sun to come up so they could go to the cemetery to bury my brother and my cousin, a neighbor, who we barely knew, stopped and asked them if they had a coffin for the children. My parents told him that they were planning on wrapping them up in a blanket. He told them to wait for him and see if he could do something about it. He came back not too long after that with a coffin big enough for both children to fit in it. My parents told him that they did not have money to pay for it and he told them that it was a gift from him. This is just one example of so many people who showed kindness to us.

A couple of days after the earthquake in Nicaragua, my maternal grandfather came to pick us up in a big truck. He lived in San Isidro, which is a small town about 120 kilometers (75 miles) north of Managua. My mother, my baby sister, and I stayed with my grandfather. Almost every day, we would go to the town's main plaza and stand in line there. We would receive all sorts of things—most of the time it was food, other times we would get clothes, toiletries, or medicine. I felt reverence and gratitude every time we went there. In everything we received, I could feel the goodness and the love of the people who had donated all those items and of those who handed them down to us. I felt safe and protected. Those items came from different parts of the world and were given by people who were helping us even though they did not know us personally. Back then I did not understand what charity was, but this experience had a great impact on me. The generosity we show makes a difference in other people, and they are able to feel God's love through us.

As we realize how much we need each other in our mortal journey, we can all be more active participants in our ward or branch kaleidoscope—a place where we all fit in, and where we are all needed.

Every one of our paths is different, yet we walk them together. Our path is not about what we have done or where we have been; it is about where we are going and what we are becoming, in unity. When we counsel together, guided by the Holy Ghost, we can see where we are and where we need to be. The Holy Ghost gives us a vision that our natural eyes cannot see, because "revelation is scattered among us"[10] and when we put that revelation together, we can see more.

As we work in unity, our purpose should be to look for and do the Lord's will; our incentive should be the love we feel for God and for our neighbor (see Matthew 22:37–40); and our greatest desire should be to "labor diligently" (Jacob 5:61), so we can prepare the way for the glorious return of our Savior. The only way we will be able to do so is "with one accord."

A friend of mine explained it this way: In music, being in accord means to be in harmony. To achieve that, we do not need to all sing the same note, and sometimes we even have to improvise. Each voice, whether high or low or in the middle, has a place to create one masterful sound. When a chord is in perfect harmony, an overtone is achieved. An overtone is a note that is not actually being played or sung, yet to a trained ear it can be heard clearly. However, if even one note is slightly out of tune, the overtone is lost and a whole chord can collapse into dissonance.

Each person in this Church has his or her very own note to sing. The wonderful thing about music is that complete, perfect harmony can be achieved by listening intently for the overtone, or the Spirit. Developing an ear for the overtone does take time and practice, but by focusing on hearing this tone—or in our lives, by focusing on feeling the Spirit—we can tune our note to align with that of Christ's.

Like the monarch butterflies, let us continue on our journey together in purpose, each of us with our own attributes and contributions, working to make this a more beautiful and fruitful world—one small step at a time and in harmony with God's commandments.

Let us unite our faith and our desire to know God's will for each of us. Our Lord Jesus Christ has promised us that when we are gathered together in His name, He is in the midst of us (see Matthew 18:20). I testify that He lives, and that He was resurrected on a beautiful spring morning to offer us the gift of immortality. He is the Monarch above all monarchs, "the King of kings, and [the] Lord of lords" (1 Timothy 6:15).

May we be one in the Father and in His Begotten Son, as we are guided by the Holy Ghost.

WE CAN REACH FOR THE SAVIOR WHEN WE KNIT OUR HEARTS TOGETHER IN UNITY AND LOVE WITH ALL THOSE AROUND US.

NOTES

1. An interesting fact about monarch butterflies is that it takes up to three generations to make the trip northward to Canada. However, a "super generation" makes the whole trip southward to Mexico, spends the winter there, and makes the first lap back north. See "Flight of the Butterflies" (video, 2012); "'Flight': A Few Million Creatures That Could," WBUR News, Sept. 28, 2012, wbur.org.

2. See "Why Do Monarchs Form Overnight Roosts during Fall Migration?," learner.org/jnorth/tm/monarch/sl/17/text.html.

3. See "What Is a Group of Butterflies Called?," amazingbutterflies.com /frequentlyaskedquestions.htm. See also "kaleidoscope," merriam-webster .com. *Kaleidoscope* comes from the Greek *kalos* (beautiful) and *eidos* (form).

4. See "The Family: A Proclamation to the World," *Ensign*, Nov. 2010, 129.

5. See Acts 2:1, 46; 4:24; 5:12; 8:6; 12:20; 15:25; 19:29. See also Philippians 2:2; 1 Nephi 10:13; 3 Nephi 11:15–17, 27–28; 17:9; Doctrine and Covenants 104:62.

6. Some of the things that the Saints did in Jerusalem: chose a new Apostle and seven men of honest report, and supported them (see Acts 1:26; 6:3–5); gathered together on the day of Pentecost (see Acts 2:1); testified of Jesus Christ (Acts 2:22–36; 3:13–26; 4:10, 33; 5:42); called people to repentance and baptized them (see Acts 2:38–41); continued in fellowship and breaking of bread, and in prayers (see Act 2:42); were together and had everything in common (see Acts 2:44–46; 4:34–35); attended the temple (see Acts 2:46); ate their meat with gladness and singleness of heart (see Acts 2:46); praised God and found favor with all people (see Acts 2:47); were obedient to the faith (see Acts 6:7); gave themselves continually to prayer and the ministry of the word (see Acts 6:4). Some of the things that the Saints did on the American continent: preached the gospel of Christ (see 3 Nephi 28:23); formed a church of Christ (see 4 Nephi 1:1); baptized people (see 4 Nephi

1:1); every man dealt justly one with another (see 4 Nephi 1:2); had all things in common among them (see 4 Nephi 1:3); rebuilt cities (see 4 Nephi 1:7–9); were married (see 4 Nephi 1:11); walked after the commandments that they received from the Lord (see 4 Nephi 1:12); continued in fasting and prayer (see 4 Nephi 1:12); met together often to pray and hear the word of the Lord (see 4 Nephi 1:12).

7. Some of the blessings that the Saints received in Jerusalem: they were filled with the Holy Ghost (see Acts 2:4; 4:31); they received the gift of tongues and prophecy and spoke the wonderful works of God (see Acts 2:4–18); many wonders and signs were done by the Apostles (see Acts 1:43); miracles happened (see Acts 3:1–10; 5:18–19; 6:8, 15); more people joined the Church (see Acts 2:47; 5:14).   Some of the blessings that the Saints received on the American continent: people were converted unto the Lord (see 3 Nephi 28:23; 4 Nephi 1:2); a generation was blessed (see 3 Nephi 28:23); there were no contentions and disputations among them (see 4 Nephi 1:2, 13, 15, 18); there were no rich and poor (see 4 Nephi 1:3); they were all made free and partakers of the heavenly gift (see 3 Nephi 1:3); there was peace in the land (see 3 Nephi 1:4); mighty miracles happened (see 4 Nephi 1:5, 13); the Lord did prosper them exceedingly (see 4 Nephi 1:7, 18); they did wax strong, did multiply exceedingly fast, and became exceedingly fair and delightsome (see 4 Nephi 1:10); they were blessed according to the multitude of promises made to them by the Lord (see 4 Nephi 1:11); there was no contention in the land, because of the love of God which did dwell in the hearts of the people (see 4 Nephi 1:15); there were no envyings, nor strifes, nor tumults, nor whoredoms, nor lyings, nor murders, nor any manner of lasciviousness; and surely there could not be a happier people among all the people who had been created by the hand of God (see 4 Nephi 1:16); there were no robbers, nor murderers, neither were there Lamanites, nor any manner of -ites; but they were in one, the children of Christ, and heirs to the kingdom of God (see 4 Nephi 1:17); the Lord blessed them in all their doings (see 4 Nephi 1:18).

8. Jean B. Bingham, "That Your Joy Might Be Full," *Ensign*, Nov. 2017, 85.

9. Jeffrey R. Holland, "Emissaries to the Church," *Ensign*, Nov. 2016, 62.

10. Neil L. Andersen, in Adam C. Olson, "Handbook Training Emphasizes Work of Salvation," *Ensign*, Apr. 2011, 68.

THE POWER OF
THE BOOK OF MORMON

How blessed are we to be members of The Church of Jesus Christ of Latter-day Saints! We are in the dispensation of the fulness of times;[1] the windows of heaven are open; and the Lord blesses us with revelation at the general level of the Church, and at the personal level of our lives.[2] This is a living Church presided over by a living prophet, President Russell M. Nelson, through whom the Lord reveals His will to us.

Yet, because we live in a fallen world, we are subject to all types of tribulation and distress. Just as Joseph Smith did, we live in a time of confusion, of strife, of crying, of tumult, and of contest. We are in the midst of a "war of words and [a] tumult of opinions."[3] We are surrounded by wickedness and iniquity. And, as we go through our mortal existence, sometimes we find ourselves amid tribulation and sorrow as we experience mortality.

Have you ever felt discouraged and inadequate?

Do you feel overwhelmed by the massive amount of information that surrounds you and the conflicting voices that pull you in different directions?

Do you have questions and longings in your heart?

Have you ever looked up to heaven and asked: *Heavenly Father, can you help me?*

We all feel like that from time to time. We struggle to find or remember our place and our purpose. At times, we may look at the future and feel that we do not have what it takes to face it. Other times, we may even look at the next day, or the next week, and be overwhelmed with fear.

During those moments, it may be difficult to believe that when we reach up to the Savior and turn our heart to Him, He has the power to strengthen or heal us. But when we turn to Him, we realize anew that our Heavenly Father has given us the means to face all that opposition and to feel joy in this life, despite the hardships that we may encounter. President Russell M. Nelson gave us the key when he said that "in coming days, it will not be possible to survive spiritually without the guiding, directing, comforting, and constant influence of the Holy Ghost."[4]

We should probably ask ourselves: How can I have the constant influence of the Holy Ghost so I can survive spiritually as President Nelson suggested?

The answer to that question is often found in the small and simple things we can incorporate into our daily lives. Those repeated practices empower us to make righteous decisions every day, so the Spirit can dwell with us. One such practice is the consistent study of the Book of Mormon. Our prophets have emphasized over and over the power that this book has and the importance of studying it daily.

President Thomas S. Monson implored us "to prayerfully study and ponder the Book of Mormon each day." He promised us that "as we do so, we will be in a position to hear the voice of the Spirit, to resist temptation, to overcome doubt and fear, and to receive heaven's help in our lives."[5]

President Russell M. Nelson taught us that "the full power of the gospel of Jesus Christ is contained in the Book of Mormon." He added: "When I think of the Book of Mormon, I think of the word power. The truths of the Book of Mormon have the *power* to heal, comfort, restore, succor, strengthen, console, and cheer our souls."[6]

I know personally that the truths found in the Book of Mormon have the power to change us, the power to draw us closer to Jesus Christ, the power to help us overcome the tribulations we may face in our lives, and the power to bring joy to us as we obey divine laws.

My husband Carlos joined The Church of Jesus Christ of Latter-day Saints in Mexico, together with his family, when he was nine years old. Due to various circumstances, most of his family did not remain active in the Church. However, Carlos did not forget how he felt when the missionaries visited his childhood home.

Years later, at age twenty-three, he moved to the United States and lived with his brother. They were occasionally visited by members and missionaries, and they kept in their apartment a copy of the Book of Mormon, which, for a long time, basically just gathered dust.

When Carlos was twenty-seven years old, he broke up with a girlfriend, and felt devastated. He then remembered how he had felt in his childhood when the Holy Ghost testified of the truth of the gospel of Jesus Christ to his young heart. He finally reached up to the Book of Mormon and opened it. As he started reading, something amazing happened: he could not stop. Back then, he had two jobs and not much spare time, but instead of eating during his breaks, he continued reading the Book of Mormon.

An interesting detail about Carlos's story is that all of this happened when the soccer extravaganza of the 1990 FIFA World Cup was going on. Those who know my husband well know how much he loves and enjoys soccer, and how important this every-four-year event is to him. Nevertheless, he completely ignored the World Cup because he was captivated by the Book of Mormon so much that he finished reading it in two weeks with the little spare time he had.

He has said to me: "As I started reading about Nephi and his family, I immediately related to him because I always tried to be the peacemaker in my family whenever there were conflicts (which, by the way, happen in every family). Nephi had a sincere desire 'to know the things that [his] father had seen, and believing that the Lord was able to make them known unto [him, he pondered in his] heart' (1 Nephi 11:1). Because of that honest desire, Nephi received his own witness of the reality of the Lord Jesus Christ and saw a vision that prepared him for what lay ahead. Somehow, I knew that the same thing could happen to me on a personal level."

Carlos continued: "I felt that every invitation to repent was given to me personally. The words of Nephi, Jacob, King Benjamin, Mosiah, Abinadi, and all the prophets in the Book of Mormon, and their witness of the divine mission of Jesus Christ, touched my heart in a profound way. As I read how Alma the Younger described his anguish as he remembered his sins, I felt the same way. My soul was tormented with pain. Similarly, when I read of the joy that Alma felt as he remembered 'to have heard [his] father prophesy unto the people concerning the coming of one Jesus Christ, a Son of God, to atone for the sins of the world' (Alma 36:17), I was overwhelmed with joy and the hope that I could also be forgiven."

As Carlos read the Book of Mormon, he had a change of heart and became a new man. He came back to church every Sunday, again renewing the covenant he had made in his childhood. By that simple act of faith of reaching up to the Savior by reading the Book of Mormon, he discovered a whole universe of truth and light in his life.

Something similar happened to me when I was twenty-six years old. I vividly remember the feelings of peace and comfort that I had as I followed the missionaries' invitation to start reading the Book of Mormon. At that time, a recurrent promise from the Lord found in the book stood out to me: "Inasmuch as ye shall keep my commandments ye shall prosper in the land" (2 Nephi 1:20). I had never heard that concept before in my life! What a beautiful promise! The Lord is assuring us that if we are obedient to His commandments, we will be blessed and prosper, both temporally and eternally.

Does that mean that we need to be perfect? No! We do not have to be perfect in every aspect of our life! We just need to have a sincere desire to know and to obey, like Nephi or like Carlos did. What needs to be exact is our desire to obey. If we strive to be obedient, through the Holy Ghost we will receive assurances from the Lord that He is pleased with our efforts. Please remember His promise: "Inasmuch as ye shall keep the commandments of God ye shall prosper in the land; and ye shall [not] be cut off from his presence" (Alma 36:30; see also Alma 37:13).

Unfailingly, each time we diligently search the Book of Mormon, we find simple patterns that we can follow in our lives as we face difficult situations.

In 2018, President Nelson pointed out to us: "Our message to the world is simple and sincere: we invite all of God's children on both sides of the veil to come unto their Savior, receive the blessings of the holy temple, have enduring joy, and qualify for eternal life."[7]

A big part of the beauty and power of the gospel of Jesus Christ lies in its simplicity, and as we strive to live it and to share its good news in a simple and sincere way, we will be instruments in the hands of the Lord to bring more souls to His fold.

One of the basic and simple principles of the gospel is faith.

"Faith is a principle of action and of power. . . [and to] lead to salvation, it must be centered in the Lord Jesus Christ."[8]

If we have faith in Christ, we believe in Him as the Son of God, the Only Begotten of the Father in the Flesh; we accept Him as our Savior and Redeemer and follow His teachings; and we believe that our sins can be forgiven through His Atonement.[9]

In the scriptures we find many examples of people who exercised faith in Jesus Christ, and because of that, they and others were blessed immensely.

One of the examples in the Book of Mormon is the brother of Jared, who was "highly favored of the Lord" and who with his family and friends obeyed the Lord's command to go into the wilderness, where man had never been. And the Lord went before them and gave directions about where they should travel, being directed continually by His hand. And the Lord said: "Go to work and build, after the manner of barges which ye have built."

And they went to work and built the barges "according to the instructions of the Lord." When the brother of Jared saw that there would be no light in the vessels, he came unto the Lord for help, and the Lord responded: "What will ye that I should do that ye may have light in your vessels?" And the brother of Jared went to the mount and did molten out of a rock sixteen stones; and they were white and clear, even as transparent glass. And he carried them to the Lord, saying: "O Lord, thou hast given us a commandment that we must call upon thee, that from thee we may receive according to our desires . . . Touch these stones, O Lord, with thy finger, and prepare them that they may shine forth in darkness." And the Lord touched the stones one by one with His finger. And the veil was taken from off the eyes of the brother of Jared, and he saw the finger of the Lord, after which the Lord showed Himself unto him because of his great faith (see Ether 1:34–3:6).

All of us find ourselves in similar situations to those of the brother of Jared. Ours may be different in degree, but they are still similar. Through His prophet, the Lord has asked us to go and minister one to another in a new, holier way. He has asked us to go forth into a wilderness where we have never been before. In our day, He has commanded us to do difficult things in the way that the brother of Jared was commanded to build barges according to His instructions. And, throughout the whole journey, He goes before us, and His hand directs us continually.

The Lord has asked us to go to work. However, when we stumble across a problem we cannot solve, He typically does not give us the whole answer, but rather He expects us to melt our own stones. He expects us to bring Him the most white, clear, and transparent stones we can, within our own capacity and according to our circumstances. He also expects us to call upon Him and ask Him to touch our stones with His finger, so they can shine in the darkness.

If we act in faith and give the Lord our best offering each day, He touches our stones in miraculous ways, He manifests Himself unto us in unexpected ways, and He blesses us immensely.

How blessed we are to have within our reach this testament of

Jesus Christ and to know that it is "the word of God" (Articles of Faith 1:8)! From beginning to end, this sacred book of scripture testifies of Jesus Christ and of His divine mission.

The Book of Mormon was written for us and for our time, and in it we find messages addressed to us in these latter days. As I read the Book of Mormon, I love finding those passages that are written specifically for *me*, and for *you* . . . for *us*.

For example, from the very beginning, in the first chapter of the First Book of Nephi, in the last verse of that chapter, Nephi wrote: "But behold, I, Nephi, will show unto *you* that the tender mercies of the Lord are over all those whom he hath chosen, because of their faith, to make them mighty even unto the power of deliverance" (1 Nephi 1:20; emphasis added). When he says, "I . . . will show unto *you*," who is he speaking to? To *you*! To *me*! That is how personal the Book of Mormon is. That is how personal the scriptures are. That is how personal the gospel of Jesus Christ is. It is for *you*! It is for *me*! It is for *each of us*!

And, yes, it is true! As we read the Book of Mormon, we can see, we can feel, and we can know for ourselves that the tender mercies of the Lord are over all of those whom He has chosen, because of their faith, to make them mighty, even unto the power of deliverance.

What does the last chapter of the Book of Mormon contain? First, a powerful exhortation to you, and to me—to us—to read it, and ask God, the Eternal Father, in the name of Christ, if the contents of the record are true. This invitation is followed by a promise that if we ask with a sincere heart, with real intent, having faith in Christ, He will manifest the truth of it unto us, by the power of the Holy Ghost, because by the power of the Holy Ghost, we may know the truth of all things (see Moroni 10:4–5).

Then, in the last verses of that last chapter, we find another exhortation and another promise. It says: "Come unto Christ, and be perfected in him, and deny yourselves of all ungodliness; and if ye shall deny yourselves of all ungodliness, and love God with all your might, mind and strength, then is his grace sufficient for you, that by his grace ye may be perfect in Christ; and if by the grace of God ye are perfect in Christ, ye can in nowise deny the power of God. And again, if ye by the grace of God are perfect in Christ, and deny not his power, then are ye sanctified in Christ by the grace of God, through the shedding of the blood of Christ, which is in the covenant of the Father unto the remission of your sins, that ye become holy, without spot" (Moroni 10:32–33).

I invite you to look for those messages and promises that are specific for *you*, and for *me*, for *us*, in these latter days. By doing so, each of you will find guidance, assurances, answers, and, most of all, a purpose. You will get closer to God, the Spirit will be your constant companion, and you will be instruments in the Lord's hands to build His kingdom on earth, and to prepare yourselves and others, on both sides of the veil, for the glorious Second Coming of our Savior and Redeemer.

I love this! This is exciting! It is invigorating!

Here are some other treasures I have found in the Book of Mormon.

In 2 Nephi 5 we read what happened in the promised land to Nephi and those who went with him after the Lord warned him to depart from his brothers, who wanted to slay him.

In verse 27, Nephi says: "We lived after the manner of happiness." We could ask ourselves: How is it possible that they lived after the manner of happiness when they had recently separated from Nephi's brothers who sought to kill them? Was it easy for them to leave the place where they had established their home and to start all over again? Could it be possible that they did not have any tribulation? Could it be that their life was a bed of roses?

Logic tells us that it is more likely that their situation was far from ideal, and that life was not easy for them. Nevertheless, they *lived after the manner of happiness*. The next question we could ask ourselves is: What did they *do* to live after that manner of happiness?

We find the answer in verses 5 through 26 in that same chapter. This is what they did:

- They followed the counsel of their prophet, Nephi (verse 6).
- They observed the commandments of the Lord in all things (verse 10).
- They planted seeds and raised flocks, herds, and animals. In other words, they were self-reliant (verse 11).
- They studied the scriptures that they had brought with them (verse 12).

- They made preparations to defend themselves from their enemies who sought to destroy them (verse 14).
- They learned to build buildings and to work with wood, iron, and all kinds of metals and precious ores. They were industrious, and labored with their hands (verses 15, 17).
- They built a temple and worshipped God in the temple (verse 16).

In just one chapter of the Book of Mormon, we learn a practical example of working hard and having the determination to press forward in unity. We learn about the spiritual strength we can enjoy when we have unwavering faith in God. We learn that by obeying the commandments and by preparing ourselves, both temporally and spiritually, we can "live after the manner of happiness," despite the evil that surrounds us, and despite our circumstances.

Now, let me tell you something that may sound strange: "I like reading the war chapters in Alma. Please do not get me wrong. I do not like violence and wars. In fact, when I was a teenager, we had a period of political unrest in Nicaragua, my home country. My maternal grandfather and one of my uncles died because of the violence. I know firsthand of the horror of violence and war. It was a difficult time for me and my family, and it brought many people a lot of heartache and sorrow.

But the reason I like the war chapters in the Book of Mormon is because of what we can learn from them. Right now, we find ourselves in the middle of a war between good and evil. In fact, this war started in the premortal world, where our Father presented

His plan of salvation to us, and Jesus Christ covenanted to be our Savior. At that time, we used our agency and decided to follow Heavenly Father and Jesus Christ. However, Lucifer, another spirit son of God, rebelled against the plan and "sought to destroy the agency of man" (Moses 4:3), and he continues to do so.

As one example of what we can learn in the war chapters, in Alma chapter 50, we read about the way in which Moroni and the Nephites prepared themselves for war:

- They dug up heaps of earth round about all the cities, throughout all the land.
- On top of those ridges of earth, they put works of timbers built up to the height of a man, round about the cities.
- On those works of timbers, they added a frame of pickets built upon the timbers round about, and they were strong and high.
- They erected towers that overlooked those works of pickets, and they built places of security upon those towers.
- Thus, they prepared strongholds against the coming of their enemies, round about every city in all the land (see Alma 50:1–6).

They prepared themselves not only temporally, but also spiritually. They gave "heed and diligence . . . unto the word of God, which was declared unto them . . . by all those who had been ordained by the holy order of God" (Alma 49:30).

Every time we do a small and simple thing to prepare spiritually, we are protecting ourselves against "the enemy of all righteousness" (Moroni 9:6). Every time we go to our knees and offer a sincere prayer to Heavenly Father, we are adding a heap of earth to our spiritual stronghold. Every time we read the scriptures, we are adding a work of timber to our soul. Every time we honor the Sabbath and partake of the sacrament, we are adding a frame of pickets to our testimony. Every time we fast, we are freeing ourselves from bondage (see Isaiah 58:6). Every time we gather with our family and our fellow Saints and feel the Spirit together, we are fortifying ourselves against temptation. Every time we listen to the prophets' counsel, we are letting them be our watchmen up in the towers, warning us of imminent dangers.

One of the marvelous aspects of studying the scriptures is that they have a different meaning for us each time we read them. Our circumstances change, our perspectives change, and we are constantly learning, growing, and becoming. Because of that, we can look at the same passage of scripture differently every time we study it. However, one aspect is always certain and constant: every time we spend time in the scriptures, we get closer to God, our vision improves, our understanding grows, and we become a better person.

To receive revelation from heaven, we must look for it in divine sources. One of those sources is the Book of Mormon. If we study it constantly, we will receive guidance, direction, and comfort. When the prophet Lehi searched the plates that his sons brought from Jerusalem, "he was filled with the Spirit" (1 Nephi 5:17). We also can be filled with the Spirit every time we read the Book of Mormon, and the Spirit will guide us and will comfort us.

We are living in the last days, and we need to keep preparing ourselves and others for the Second Coming of our Savior. We need to help gather the children of God. President Russell M. Nelson invited the youth of the Church to be actively engaged in the cause of gathering Israel. Let us follow our prophet's invitation and be part of "the *greatest* challenge, the *greatest* cause, and the *greatest* work on earth,"[10] as he called it.

Nephi saw our days—and the need of gathering—in a vision, and wrote: "It came to pass that I, Nephi, beheld the power of the Lamb of God, that it descended upon the saints of the church of the Lamb, and upon the covenant people of the Lord, who were scattered upon all the face of the earth; and they were armed with righteousness and with the power of God in great glory" (1 Nephi 14:14).

I testify to you that the Book of Mormon was written "to the convincing of the Jew and Gentile that Jesus is the Christ, the Eternal God, manifesting himself unto all nations" (title page of the Book of Mormon).

It is my humble prayer that we can read the Book of Mormon looking for the revelation we need every day so that we can "live after the manner of happiness" personally and in our families, regardless of our circumstances; that we can read it looking for the promises found in its pages, which will give us the strength to keep going with determination; and that we can read it to draw closer to our Heavenly Father and Jesus Christ, so we can have the constant influence of the Holy Ghost and survive spiritually.

WE CAN REACH FOR THE SAVIOR BY TREASURING HIS WORD, FEASTING UPON THE SACRED BOOK OF SCRIPTURE GIVEN FOR OUR DAY, THE BOOK OF MORMON.

NOTES

1. See Ephesians 1:10; Doctrine and Covenants 112:30; 121:31; 124:41; 128:18, 20; 138:48.
2. See Russell M. Nelson, "Revelation for the Church, Revelation for our Lives," *Ensign*, May 2018, 93–96.
3. See Joseph Smith—History 1:8–11.
4. Russell M. Nelson, "Revelation for the Church, Revelation for Our Lives," *Ensign*, May 2018, 96.
5. Thomas S. Monson, "The Power of the Book of Mormon," *Ensign*, May 2017, 87.
6. Russell M. Nelson, "The Book of Mormon: What Would Your Life Be Like without It?" *Ensign*, Nov. 2017, 62.
7. Russell M. Nelson, "Let Us All Press On," *Ensign*, May 2018, 118–19
8. "Faith in Jesus Christ," Gospel Topics, topics.ChurchofJesusChrist.org.
9. See *Preach My Gospel: A Guide to Missionary Service* (2018), 122.
10. Russell M. Nelson, "Hope of Israel" (worldwide devotional for youth, June 3, 2018) broadcasts.ChurchofJesusChrist.org.

MIRACLES OF HEALING THROUGH TEMPLE ORDINANCES

We know that the work and the glory of God is "to bring to pass the immortality and eternal life of man" (Moses 1:39). Because of the Fall, we are all "in a lost and in a fallen state" (1 Nephi 10:6). President Russell M. Nelson taught, "We are all subject to sorrow and suffering, to disease and death. . . . Afflictions can come from spiritual as well as physical causes." But then, he said, "Faith, repentance, baptism, a testimony, and enduring conversion lead to the healing power of the Lord."[1]

All children of God, who are accountable for their decisions, regardless of the place, time, and circumstances in which they live or have lived, need to receive the opportunity to exercise faith in Jesus Christ, to repent, and to accept His gospel, on either side of the veil. Each of God's children needs spiritual healing, and as His disciples, we have been called to help make that possible.

In Mosiah 27:25–26 we read: "All mankind, yea, men and women, all nations, kindreds, tongues and people, must be born again; yea, born of God, changed from their carnal and fallen state, to a state of righteousness, being redeemed of God, becoming his sons and daughters; And thus they become new creatures; and unless they do this, they can in nowise inherit the kingdom of God."

Because of the Savior's atoning sacrifice, saving temple ordinances allow us and our ancestors to be born again, to be changed to a state of righteousness, to be redeemed of God, and to become new creatures.

When the scribes and Pharisees murmured against His disciples, Jesus Christ answered them, "They that are whole need not a physician; but they that are sick. I came not to call the righteous, but sinners to repentance" (Luke 5:31–32). To me, this means that we are all in need of repentance and healing, we have all made mistakes, and we have all struggled and suffered. We are all in need of the healing balm that the Savior offers.

President James E. Faust declared: "Christ is the great Physician, who rose from the dead 'with healing in his wings' (2 Nephi 25:13), while the Comforter is the agent of healing.

"The Lord has provided many avenues by which we may receive this healing influence. . . . [He] has restored temple work to the earth. It is an important part of the work of salvation for both the living and the dead. Our temples provide a sanctuary where we may go to lay aside many of the anxieties of the world. Our temples are places of peace and tranquility. In these hallowed sanctuaries God 'healeth the broken in heart, and bindeth up their wounds' [Psalm 147:3]."[2]

We hear stories of miracles of healing that occur in holy temples everywhere. We hear of faithful members who come to the temple in buses and spend all day and evening performing saving ordinances for their ancestors. We hear of dedicated youth attending the temple early in the morning before school to perform baptisms and confirmations for their ancestors and helping with different aspects of those sacred ordinances. We hear of groups of young women and young men taking public transportation after school one day each week to offer their ancestors the opportunity to be spiritually born again. We hear of families navigating in boats for hours to attend the temple to receive saving temple ordinances for themselves, so that through Jesus Christ's Atonement, they can be changed to a state of righteousness. We hear of individual members and families finding names of dear ancestors on the Sabbath and then taking those names to the temple to give those family members the opportunity to be redeemed by God. We hear of eleven-year-old boys and girls who are eager to come to the temple and who have to stand on the last step of the baptismal font because the water is too deep for them—all to give their ancestors the chance to become new creatures.

If we think about it, we realize that we all come to the temple to be spiritually healed and to give those on the other side of the veil the opportunity to be healed as well. When it comes to healing, we all need the Savior desperately. I will illustrate this with the story of two of my ancestors.

My paternal grandmother, Isabel Blanco, was born in Potosí, Nicaragua. In my memories, she is a loving, hardworking, and faithful woman. As I was growing up, she planted in my young heart the seed of faith as I saw her pray to God with fervor and as she took me to mass every Sunday to worship Jesus. However, she did not have an easy life. Among many other things that she did, when she was young, she worked as a maid for an affluent family. As was sadly common, her employer got her pregnant, and when she could no longer hide her pregnancy, she was dismissed.

My father, Noel, was born from that pregnancy, and although Potosí was a small town and everyone, including Noel, knew who his father was, Noel never had any direct contact or relationship with him.

Isabel never married, and she had two other children out of wedlock. After some time, she and her three children moved to the country's capital, Managua, looking for better employment and educational opportunities.

During his late teen years, Noel developed an addiction to alcohol. He eventually met and married my mother, Delbi Cardoza, and they had four children. Through the years, his alcoholism took a toll on their marriage. After moving to San Francisco, California, in their fifties, they separated. Unfortunately, my father died by suicide a few years later.

When my father, Noel, passed away, my mother and I were already members of The Church of Jesus Christ of Latter-day Saints. A few years after his death, all the proxy temple ordinances were performed in his behalf, except for one: the sealing ordinance. At the time, I did not dare ask my mother if she wanted to be sealed to him, because I knew how strained their relationship had been.

Then, a miracle happened. My mother had a dream in which she saw her husband Noel outside the kitchen door in their home in Managua, extending his hand to her and inviting her to come with him. She woke up with a sweet feeling in her heart. Not too long after that, she called me one day and calmly said, "I am going to be sealed to your *papá* this Saturday. You can come if you want." I replied excitedly, "Of course I want to be there!" After hanging up, I joyfully realized that I could also be sealed to them, and I made the arrangements to do so.

On a glorious Saturday morning, my mother, my husband, our son, and I knelt at a sacred temple altar and performed the living and proxy sealing ordinances that gave my parents, my deceased brother, and me the opportunity to be together forever. At that holy moment, all the bad feelings, pains, and sorrows were forgotten. We all felt the soothing and healing balm that our Savior Jesus Christ offers us through His Atonement, on both sides of the veil.

Years later, I had a dream in which I saw my father, Noel, at what seemed to be a pulpit in one of our meetinghouses. He was wearing a white shirt and a tie, and he was giving an inspiring message. In my dream, I could perceive that he was a "seasoned" leader of the Church. I do not know exactly what that dream means, but it gives me the hope that, maybe, he has accepted the gospel of Jesus Christ in the spirit world.

At some point, we also performed the temple work for my grandmother, Isabel (except for the sealing to spouse ordinance because she was not married in her life). Just think about this: a woman like Isabel, who was not treated with respect by men and who dealt with many struggles in her life, can be given the opportunity on the other side of the veil to exercise her agency and make a sacred covenant with God through a proxy ordinance in the temple. She, like all of us, is in need of increased faith, in need of repentance, in need of love, in need of sanctification—in short, in need of healing.

Looking back now, I can see that even though Noel had a difficult childhood and a damaging addiction, his love for his children was stronger than his weaknesses. When he was with us, his best qualities would come out. He was always kind to us, and I cannot remember even one occasion on which he lost his temper with his children. Because God is merciful, Noel is also given the chance to exercise faith, to repent, and to accept Jesus Christ as his Redeemer through saving ordinances performed in the holy temple. Noel, like all of us, is also in need of healing.

These are just two examples of the eternal blessings of healing that are offered to individuals and families in all of the Lord's temples around the world. As taught by President Nelson, the reason we have temples is to "invite all of God's children on both sides of the veil to come unto their Savior, receive the blessings of the holy temple, have enduring joy, and qualify for eternal life."[3]

When I think about all that needed to happen for Isabel and Noel to receive that eternal gift, I realize that it is a miracle made possible by a loving Heavenly Father and a Savior who love us with perfect love and who have called each of us to help in God's work and glory.

Elder Dale G. Renlund taught: "Family history and temple work [provide] the power to heal that which [needs] healing . . . God, in His infinite capacity, seals and heals individuals and families despite tragedy, loss, and hardship."[4]

Speaking of the gathering of Israel, President Nelson has said: "When we speak of the gathering, we are simply saying this fundamental truth: every one of our Heavenly Father's children, on both sides of the veil, deserves to hear the message of the restored gospel of Jesus Christ. They decide for themselves if they want to know more." He explained, "*Anytime* you do *anything* that helps *anyone*—on either side of the veil—take a step toward making covenants with God and receiving their essential baptismal and temple ordinances, you are helping to gather Israel. It is as simple as that."[5]

I do not know if my *abuelita* Isabel, my *papá* Noel, and the rest of my ancestors for whom temple work has been performed have accepted the gospel of Jesus Christ in the spirit world. However, I can have hope, I can exercise faith, I can make and keep covenants with God, and I can live my life in a way that will allow me to be with my ancestors "in a state of happiness which hath no end" (Mormon 7:7). When I get to the other side of the veil, if they have not yet accepted the gospel of Jesus Christ, I will make sure to teach it to them! I can't wait to give them a hug, to tell them how much I love them, to have heart-to-heart conversations that I never had with them when they were alive, and to testify to them that "Jesus is the Christ, the Eternal God" (title page of the Book of Mormon).

Sometimes, the natural man and woman in us make us think that when we are given callings in the Church, we have been called to "fix" other people. As disciples of Jesus Christ, we have not been called by Him to be "fixers" of others, and we have not been called to lecture or to scorn. We have been called to inspire, to lift, and to invite others, to be fishers of people, fishers of souls, so they receive the opportunity to be spiritually healed by Jesus Christ, our Savior and Redeemer.

In Isaiah 61, we read the Lord's words, which were also quoted by Him when He started His ministry in Jerusalem (see Luke 4:18–19). In verses 1 through 4, He declared: "The Spirit of the Lord God is upon me; because the Lord hath anointed me to preach good tidings unto the meek; he hath sent me to bind up the brokenhearted, to proclaim liberty to the captives, and the opening of the prison to them that are bound; to proclaim the acceptable year of the Lord, and the day of vengeance of our God; to comfort all that mourn; to appoint unto them that mourn in Zion, to give unto them beauty for ashes, the oil of joy for mourning, the garment of praise for the spirit of heaviness; that they might be called trees of righteousness, the planting of the Lord, that he might be glorified. And they shall build the old wastes, they shall raise up the former desolations, and they shall repair the waste cities, the desolations of many generations."

That is what we have been called to do, to "build the old wastes," to "raise up the former desolations," to "repair the waste cities."

President Nelson has taught, "The real power to heal . . . comes from God."[6] He has also given us this assurance: "The gift of resurrection is the Lord's consummate act of healing. Thanks to Him, each body will be restored to its proper and perfect frame. Thanks to Him, no condition is hopeless. Thanks to Him, brighter days are ahead, both here and hereafter. Real joy awaits each of us—on the other side of sorrow."[7]

I testify that our Heavenly Father loves each of us so much that He has provided "a way"[8] so that each of us can be physically and spiritually healed as we exercise faith in Jesus Christ, make and keep our covenants with God, and follow His commandments. I testify that Christ came to the earth "to heal the brokenhearted, to preach deliverance to the captives" (Luke 4:18), so each of us can "become holy, without spot" (Moroni 10:33).

WE CAN REACH FOR THE SAVIOR BY MAKING COVENANTS IN HIS HOLY HOUSE, SEEKING RESTORATION AND HEALING FOR US AND OUR ANCESTORS.

NOTES

1. Russell M. Nelson, "Jesus Christ—the Master Healer," *Ensign*, Nov. 2005, 85–86.
2. James E. Faust, "Spiritual Healing," *Ensign*, May 1992, 7.
3. Russell M. Nelson, "Let Us All Press On," *Ensign*, May 2018, 118–19.
4. Dale G. Renlund, "Family History and Temple Work: Sealing and Healing," *Ensign*, May 2018, 46–48.
5. Russell M. Nelson, "Hope of Israel" (worldwide youth devotional, June 3, 2018), HopeofIsrael.ChurchofJesusChrist.org.
6. Sheri Dew, *Insights from a Prophet's Life: Russell M. Nelson* (Salt Lake City: Deseret Book, 2019), 150.
7. Russell M. Nelson, "Jesus Christ—the Master Healer," *Ensign*, Nov. 2005, 87.
8. See Isaiah 42:16; 51:10; 1 Nephi 3:7; 9:6; 17:41; 22:20; 2 Nephi 8:10; 9:10; Ether 12:8; Doctrine and Covenants 132:50.

CENTRAL TO
THE CREATOR'S PLAN

We all belong to the family of God because each of us is a child of heavenly parents. We lived with Them before coming to this earth and we all have the potential to become like Them. As President Dallin H. Oaks of the Quorum of the Twelve Apostles has said, "Our theology begins with heavenly parents. Our highest aspiration is to be like Them."[1] We were born to replenish the earth with goodness, to have righteous dominion over the abundant resources we have received from God, and to be obedient to His divine laws (see Abraham 4:26–31).

Each of us also belongs to an earthly family. Regardless of our circumstances, we all have the responsibility to strengthen each member of that family.

Marriage is ordained of God; it is central to the Creator's plan and it is the means that He has created so we can be born in families and taught to walk in His ways. Although not all of us have the opportunity to marry in this life, marriage still needs to be part of our aspirations, so the eternal purposes of God for us can be accomplished.

President Henry B. Eyring once said to the women of the Church, "You cannot know when, or for what length of time, your personal mission will be focused on service in calls such as mother, leader, or ministering sister. The Lord, out of love, does not leave us the choice of the timing, duration, or sequence of our assignments. Yet you know from scripture and living prophets that all of these assignments will come, either in this life or in the next, to every daughter of God. And all of them are preparation for eternal life in loving families—'the greatest of all the gifts of God' [Doctrine and Covenants 14:7]."[2]

Even though we may not have control over the timing of getting married, we can prepare for it, knowing that eventually the day will come, either in this life or in the next. I once heard that *finding* an ideal person for us is not as important as *becoming* an ideal person for someone and for all the people around us. We could expand that to say that, as disciples of Jesus Christ, our highest desire should be to follow His example of love and "allow [Him] to transform us into the best version of ourselves."[3]

Elder Jeffrey R. Holland taught, "In a world of varied talents and fortunes that we can't always command, I think that makes even more attractive the qualities we *can* command—such qualities as thoughtfulness, patience, a kind word, and true delight in the accomplishment of another. These cost us *nothing*, and they can mean *everything* to the one who receives them."[4]

One of the most important decisions we make in life is whom to marry. Many times, we create long lists of attributes that we want in that person with whom we will spend the rest of our mortality and hopefully, our eternity. The reality is that when we marry someone, neither that person nor we are perfect. We both continue working on our perfection and in our relationship with God and with each other. It is up to each of us to become one as we raise a family and face life together.

At the time I joined the Church, I was certain that I would not remarry. The wounds of my first marriage were still fresh, and the thought of getting married again was not on my mind.

Just a few months after I was baptized into the Church, I received the calling to be the Sunday School teacher in the Gospel Principles class. I was scared since I was a new member, but the counselor in the branch presidency who interviewed me said to me, "Don't worry. There will always be people there that can help you." It ended up being a great learning experience for me as I made an honest effort to do my best in that calling.

One Sunday, as I was teaching that class, a young man started attending. His name was Carlos Aburto. He was from Mexico and about my same age. He was coming back to the Church after years of not attending. At first, we did not interact much, but over the following months, we became friends.

About a year after I met Carlos, I moved from California to Utah. I had relatives there who encouraged me to move. I felt that it would be a good environment for me to raise my son.

After two years of living in Utah, I went back to California one Christmas to see my sister. While I was there, I felt the desire to talk to and catch up with my friend Carlos. We had a conversation that lasted many hours, and it felt like I was with my best friend. We realized that we had a lot in common and that we really liked each other, and we started dating. Five months later, we got sealed in the Jordan River Temple, and my son Xavier, who was six years old at the time, was also sealed to us. We eventually had two more children, Elena and Carlos Enrique.

I feel that in society we idealize dating and marriage so much that it is hard for some of our young adults to go through life trying to be the best they can, and at the same time, preparing for marriage in the eternities. Sometimes, we romanticize the thought that we will know as soon as we meet the person we will marry that he or she is the right one.

Many of us did not fall in love at first sight and did not realize that we would marry someone until years after we met that person. In our case, Carlos and I got married three years after we met. We simply were not ready to get married sooner. We needed to grow and to learn in our separate ways before we realized that we could start a family together.

To anyone who is in the process of finding their eternal companion, I would say, do not worry so much about the unwritten rules of society. Nowadays, it seems that there are many acronyms that rule relationships. After only a few dates, we feel forced to DTR (or define the relationship), when we could be patient and give ourselves more time to get to know each other. Do not stress over specific scripts or ways of doing things. Do not overthink dates. There is not a mold; there is not a single pattern. The Holy Ghost does not have a script. Many times, He will just whisper to us, "It is time to go home," and we need to listen to those un-scripted, individual-to-us promptings. If you are making a sincere effort to follow divine laws and to be respectful of others, the Holy Ghost will guide you and you will know what to do.

Sometimes we feel that we need to follow a script through NPC conversations (or non-player-character conversations) like in video games. When we do that, the interaction is forced. Be your-self, treat others like they are already your friends, and the con-versation will be more natural. Focus on the other person and not on yourself. Ask follow-up questions, listen with the desire to get to know him or her, and express your feelings and points of view. Show genuine interest, and before you know it, you will have made a new friend and you will become a better friend.

If your friendship with someone of the opposite gender turns romantic and you fall in love, that will be a wonderful bonus! Do not be afraid to fall in love and to get married. Eternal marriage is such an important part of the plan of salvation. It is the beginning of an eternal family and the beginning of a journey that allows us to love God and our eternal companion in a divine way.

For me, Carlos has been a marvelous blessing. I consider him a miracle in my life. He has been a great father to my three children. He fears God and strives to be a faithful disciple of Christ. Our marriage has had the foundation of our faith and testimony of the gospel. Together, we have tried to serve the Lord as faithfully as we can.

As I look back now, I realize that our life together has not been easy. We have struggled through the sometimes-tedious routine of everyday life. When our three children were little, Carlos and I both worked outside our home. We had to juggle our responsibilities with raising our children, serving in Church callings, providing for our family's needs, and keeping our house so it could be a haven where the Spirit could dwell.

I remember the frustrations of coming home from work, getting a piece of frozen meat from the freezer, and staring at it with the thought, "What am I supposed to do with this? How am I going to make a decent meal out of this hard piece of ice?"

Other times, we barely had time to prepare a quick tuna salad sandwich for dinner so we could pick up some of the youth from our ward and still make it on time to a youth activity, a soccer game, a piano lesson, and so forth.

And yet, there have been many constants in our family life that I feel have helped us as we have strived to raise our family in truth and righteousness. One of them has been our commitment to have dinner together with our children as much as possible. Gathering around our sacred dinner table to thank God for His many blessings and to ask Him for His protection and guidance has been like a daily stepping-stone in our journey together. The conversations about our day, the reflections on the blessings we receive each day, the nurturing food that strengthens our body and delights our soul, the sense of humor that gives us a chance to decompress, and the safety of our love for each other have been like a glue that keeps us rooted to the gospel of Jesus Christ.

As our children were growing up, we tried to be diligent with reading the scriptures and having home evenings with them, although I cannot say that we were always perfectly consistent, and sometimes our attempts were disastrous. It would take us more than a year to read the whole Book of Mormon together because we would read just a few verses at a time.

Also, attending the temple as a couple was quite a feat, and we would find comfort in knowing that "to every thing there is a season, and a time to every purpose under the heaven" (Ecclesiastes 3:1).

We strived to teach our children of the joy we feel when we make a sincere effort to follow God's commandments. For example, paying our tithing was always important for us, and we wanted our children to grow up with the desire to obey that divine law. While they were too young to understand percentages, we would just give them one dollar and help them fill out the tithing slip. We would also explain to them that the money we give as tithing is used to build meetinghouses and temples, among other things.

When our youngest son, Carlos Enrique, was about fifteen years old, one day he told me, "When I was little and I paid my tithing, I was certain that each time I gave a dollar, a whole meetinghouse was being built with that one dollar. Isn't that silly?"

His story truly touched my heart, and I asked him, "That is so beautiful! Did you picture those meetinghouses in your mind?"

He replied, "Yes! They were beautiful, and there were millions of them!"

There is so much we can learn from a child's heart. Their joy in simplicity, their desire to give their all and to live every moment at their fullest, are things that we adults need to feel more often. Jesus Christ told us: "Verily I say unto you, Except ye be converted, and become as little children, ye shall not enter into the kingdom of heaven" (Matthew 18:3).

In our family life, we can all be like little children and do the small and simple things that get us closer to God, trusting and knowing that great things will come to pass through the grace of Christ.

When I look back, I wish we would have done some things differently with our children, but we cannot judge our past mistakes with today's knowledge; we can only learn from the past and make the determination to be better today than we were yesterday.

Jean B. Bingham, Relief Society General President, has taught: "Unity is essential to the divine work we are privileged and called to do, but it doesn't just happen. It takes effort and time to really counsel together—to listen to one another, understand others' viewpoints, and share experiences—but the process results in more inspired decisions. Whether at home or in our Church responsibilities, the most effective way to fulfill our divine potential is to work together, blessed by the power and authority of the priesthood in our differing yet complementary roles."[5]

Regardless of our circumstances, our home is the laboratory where we can apply the truths we believe and the doctrine we follow. It is the place for us to love, forgive, ask for forgiveness, learn, grow, progress, and reach our divine potential.

WE CAN REACH FOR THE SAVIOR
AS WE NURTURE AND STRENGTHEN
LOVING FAMILY RELATIONSHIPS.

NOTES

1. Dallin H. Oaks, "Apostasy and Restoration," *Ensign*, May 1995, 84.
2. Henry B. Eyring, "Covenant Women in Partnership with God," *Ensign*, Nov. 2019, 71.
3. Russell M. Nelson, "We Can Do Better and Be Better," *Ensign*, May 2019, 67.
4. Jeffrey R. Holland, "How do I love thee?," *New Era*, October 2003, 6.
5. Jean B. Bingham, "United in Accomplishing God's Work," *Ensign*, May 2020, 62.

GREAT SHALL BE THE PEACE OF THY CHILDREN

Some years ago, my husband Carlos and I were called to teach the temple preparation course in our ward. As part of our calling, our bishop asked us to teach the seventeen-year-old young women and young men about preparing to enter the temple. As we introduced the first lesson to our eager students, we mentioned to them that in the temple we learn about the great plan of salvation. One of the young men, with a look of relief on his face, exclaimed, "Really?! Is that what we learn in the temple? That makes me feel so much better!"

His reaction made a deep impression on me, and made me wonder, did Carlos and I ever tell our children that in the temple we learn about the plan of salvation? I honestly could not remember what we told them and what we did not tell them about the temple. But I knew for sure that we probably did not tell them enough, and I wished I had a second chance. Then I remembered: *Wait a minute! I do have a second chance!* In His infinite mercy, the Lord is constantly giving us second chances! I will have a second chance and a third chance, and many other chances, with each of my grandchildren! What is more amazing is that I constantly have new chances not only with my family but also with "the rising generation,"[1] with any young person in my sphere of influence.

More recently, I had the opportunity to visit the Paris France Temple with my family. In the temple visitors' center, we were welcomed by missionaries. Among other things, they showed us a beautiful scale model of the temple and gave the same overview that they give to all visitors, including those who are not of our faith. In a simple yet powerful and profound way, they told us about the different rooms in the temple and what happens inside each of them.

Without using the exact words spoken in the temple and without revealing any of the sacred information that we who have been endowed in the temple have promised not to disclose, those missionaries gave us a magnificent and comprehensive summary of the enlightening and empowering things we do within its walls. Among other insights, they told us that the temple is a place where we learn that God has a plan and that we are part of that plan. They also told us that in the house of the Lord we make specific promises to keep God's laws and to strive to become like Him. They beautifully described the joy we can feel if we keep those promises. They also mentioned that Heavenly Father promises us His blessings in return and that He always keeps His promises.

Once again, I asked myself, *Why has it never occurred to me to teach my children about the temple in a similarly profound and simple way? Why have I denied my children the blessing of hearing more from me the wonderful truths I have learned and the important promises I have made with God in His house through the years?*

When Jesus Christ visited the Nephites in the American continent, He told them, "And all thy children shall be taught of the Lord; and great shall be the peace of thy children" (3 Nephi 22:13).

When our children are taught of the Lord, they have great peace, the peace that comes only from Him. The Lord has said, "Peace I leave with you, my peace I give unto you: not as the world giveth, give I unto you" (John 14:27). For our children to have great peace, they need to be taught of the Lord, they need to be taught about His peace, His infinite Atonement, and His divine gifts of grace and mercy, in every way possible.

I have felt in my heart that when the Lord says "thy children" or that when our prophets, seers, and revelators talk about "our children," they are not referring to only the children who are related to us by bone and blood, by marriage, or by adoption. I feel that they are referring to all of our children—in other words, the rising generation. I feel that they are referring to all the children, the teenagers, and the young adults—anyone in those groups on whom we can have righteous influence. Maybe it means anyone who is younger than us, or, perhaps, it also includes those who are older, because we all belong to the family of God, we all need to be taught of the Lord, and we are all in need of great peace.

Unfortunately, some young souls in the rising generation are being lured away from the gospel of Jesus Christ, and some of them are not feeling that peace that comes from the Lord. They are bombarded with a myriad of information on the internet, on social media, in music, and through many other means. They are hearing and reading negative comments, distorted depictions, and disrespectful and degrading descriptions about what happens inside the sacred walls of our temples and about many other sacred aspects of the gospel of Jesus Christ. For some, going to the temple for the first time is an uncomfortable experience, when it should be a positive one. They should be wanting to go back again and again, but for all these reasons, their testimonies and their faith in Jesus Christ are being undermined. Some of them have questions, and they are not getting the answers through the right sources.

If the temple is such a great source of truth, guidance, revelation, and peace for us, the ones who have been "endowed with power from on high" (D&C 38:32), could we possibly share more of that source of peace and strength with our children? If bringing people to the temple is the ultimate goal of everything we do in The Church of Jesus Christ of Latter-day Saints, if sealing families together in God's family is our most sublime motive, if helping all of God's children receive the blessings promised to Abraham is our highest aspiration, if helping each other prepare to be in the presence of God is our greatest desire, could we possibly make the temple more relevant in our everyday conversations with the rising generation?

With all the protection that we have put around the sacred things we learn, feel, and do in the temple, I wonder if we have gone to an extreme—an almost complete silence that is stopping us from teaching all of our children about the temple in a more relatable and accessible way, so they can have greater peace in their hearts and be better prepared to face the world.

After two days of teaching and ministering to the Nephites of all ages, including their children, the Lord returned on the third day and once again taught and ministered to them, filling their hearts with spiritual truths. As a result, their children "yea, even babes did open their mouths and utter marvelous things" (3 Nephi 26:16).

Of this extraordinary event, Sister Michaelene Grassli, former Primary General President, said: "Because of miraculous instructions, blessings, and attention [the Nephites] and their children received, *righteousness was perpetuated* by their children's children for many generations.

"Let us not underestimate the *capacity* and *potential power* of today's children to perpetuate righteousness. No group of people in the Church is as receptive to the truth, both in efficiency of learning and with the greatest degree of retention. No group is as vulnerable to erroneous teaching, and no group suffers more from neglect. . . . We, the adults of the world, must open the way for them. Our . . . children worldwide deserve to be 'remembered and nourished by the good word of God, to keep them in the right way' [Moroni 6:4]."[2]

It is impressive to me to see how the young members of The Church of Jesus Christ of Latter-day Saints respond in remarkable ways to the invitations extended by our leaders to step up and to be active participants in the work of salvation and exaltation.

For example, in 2011, Elder David A. Bednar extended an invitation to the rising generation "to learn about and experience the Spirit of Elijah." He then gave them this profound promise: "As you respond in faith to this invitation, your hearts shall turn to the fathers. . . . Your testimony of and conversion to the Savior will become deep and abiding. And I promise you will be protected against the intensifying influence of the adversary. As you participate in and love this holy work, you will be safeguarded in your youth and throughout your lives."[3]

This invitation ignited a continuous wave of young hearts turning to their fathers (see Malachi 4:6)—not only to their earthly fathers and ancestors but also to their spiritual fathers, both our Heavenly Father and our Savior Jesus Christ. Our young friends not only have turned their hearts, but they have also helped us turn ours.

In 2012, President Thomas S. Monson announced that the minimum age for missionary service would be lowered, and he encouraged "all young men who [were] worthy and . . . physically able and mentally capable to respond to the call to serve. He also reminded our young women that although they were "not under the same mandate to serve as the young men . . . they make a valuable contribution as missionaries," and their service was welcome.[4]

Again, a wave of righteousness and consecration soon began in the Church, as the rising generation responded to that call from the prophet and embarked in the service of God by the thousands.

In December 2017, in a letter from the First Presidency, it was announced that young women could assist in the temple baptistry and that priests (the young men between sixteen and eighteen) could officiate in baptisms for the dead in the temple.[5] Similarly, in October 2019, it was announced that any baptized member of the Church could act as a witness for the baptism of a living person, and that anyone with a temple recommend could serve as a witness for a proxy baptism in the temple.[6]

Once more, our young friends are fulfilling these new responsibilities with love and humility, and they are helping their ancestors and our ancestors on the other side of the veil to receive saving ordinances.

In April 2018, President Russell M. Nelson announced "a newer, holier approach to caring for and ministering to others"[7] for Young Women, Young Men, members of Relief Society, and members of the Melchizedek Priesthood quorums.

Once again, our young women and young men are responding to the call. The work done by the sisters of the Relief Society and by the brothers of the Melchizedek Priesthood quorums is being magnified, expanded, and elevated by our young women and young men, who are stepping up and ministering to others in inspired ways all around the world.

In June 2018, President Nelson invited "*every* young woman and *every* young man between the ages of 12 and 18 in The Church of Jesus Christ of Latter-day Saints to enlist in the youth battalion of the Lord to help gather Israel."[8]

As expected, our young women and our young men—and members of all ages—have hearkened to our prophet's voice. They have been prayerfully and actively finding ways to help gather Israel. They share the light of the gospel of Jesus Christ with their friends in their school, their neighborhoods, and online.

In September 2018, in a devotional for young adults, Elder Quentin L. Cook promised them that studying the history of the Church will deepen their faith and their desire to live the gospel more fully.[9]

If the rising generation responds to Elder Cook's invitation as they have responded to previous invitations from our called leaders, we will soon have many young Church historians around us, and we will have the wonderful opportunity to learn from them. They will teach us, and they will tutor us.

In the scriptures, we learn that Samuel, David, Nephi, Captain Moroni, Mormon, and even Joseph Smith, the Prophet of this dispensation—along with many others—were entrusted by God with sacred truths and responsibilities at a young age, and they responded to the call.

Our young friends step up, they respond to inspired invitations from our leaders, and they are willing to consecrate themselves to the Lord's work. If we treat them as "agents unto themselves" (D&C 58:28) who can act for themselves instead of being acted upon (see 2 Nephi 2:26), they will become agents unto themselves, and they will step up. As we teach them pure doctrine with love, they understand it, they internalize it, and they find ways to apply it to their lives and use it to bless the lives of others.

Knowing that our young friends in the Church have divine potential and the desire to grow and learn, these questions have been pounding in my heart: What would I teach about the temple to my grandchildren and to any young person with whom I could have some influence? What would I say to the "pure in heart" (Jacob 3:1–3) about the house of the Lord?

Considering our prophet's emphasis on making the home even more the center of teaching, learning, studying, and living the gospel of Jesus Christ, I wonder if we could share more insights about the temple with the rising generation and with our loved ones during those holy conversations we have around our sacred dinner table or when we are ministering to each other.

I am not implying that we should speak lightly and carelessly about the temple. However, I feel that if we follow the Spirit, if we do not quote the exact words used in the temple, if we do not disclose the information that we have covenanted not to, and if we take into account the heart and the intentions of those with whom we are interacting, we could probably help them be better prepared for when their time comes to make covenants with the Lord in His sacred temple.

So, what would I tell them? Without dumping a lot of information at once, and depending on their understanding, I could probably tell them the following, among other things:

- The temple is a place where we prepare ourselves to be back in the presence of God.
- In the temple we learn about the plan of salvation and the divine mission of Jesus Christ in that plan.
- In the temple we participate in ordinances, both for ourselves and for our ancestors.
- To prepare ourselves for higher promises and blessings in the temple, we are symbolically cleansed from sin. We are then anointed on the head with oil and blessed to become more like God and Jesus Christ. This ceremony is symbolic of the washing and anointing of Aaron and his sons as described in the Bible.
- Part of the instruction we receive in the temple is done through a film and audio recording. We are taught about the creation of the earth, the role of the Savior, Adam and Eve, the Fall, and how God's plan redeems us from the Fall because of Christ's sacrifice. We also learn about the promises we will make with God:

  ○ We promise to obey all of God's commandments that we learn from the scriptures and prophets.
  ○ We promise God that we will sacrifice our own will

for His. Sacrificing in this way reminds us of Jesus Christ's sacrifice for us.

- o We promise to strive to live as Jesus did by focusing on holy and pure practices. We promise to speak respectfully of the Lord's servants and not to make light of sacred things, use offensive humor, or use God's name inappropriately.

- o We promise to have no sexual relations before marriage, and to be completely faithful to our spouse once married.

- o We promise to be willing to give everything we have—or will have—to God to help accomplish His work. This includes our time, our talents, and everything He blesses us with.

- In the temple everyone wears white clothing, which is symbolic of purity and equality.

- Once we are endowed in the temple, we wear sacred garments under our outer clothing that have deep religious significance. President Nelson has explained, "Just as the Savior exemplified the need to endure to the end, we wear the garment faithfully as part of the enduring armor of God."[10]

- In the temple, marriage ceremonies are performed in beautiful rooms where a man and a woman kneel together at an altar and make promises with God and each other. Couples are married in the temple for more than this life; they are married for all eternity.

- We are expected to center our lives on Jesus Christ and

the promises He asks us to make to God in the temple. Therefore, we sometimes say that our lives are centered on the temple or that the temple is a focus of our faith.

- Through the ordinances available in the temple, we can be with God and our families forever, regardless of when they lived, how long they lived, or whether they were able to make these temple promises during their own lives.

I would also tell them that as we make promises to our Heavenly Father, He promises us that we can return to live with Him and become like Him. He promises us that we can be with our families forever and enjoy greater blessings than we can imagine.

How grateful I am for the gift of repentance and for second chances. The Lord Jesus Christ in His loving mercy meets us where we are and takes us by the hand if we let Him. Each day, He gives us the opportunity to repent, to progress, to improve, and to draw nearer to Him.

"We talk of Christ, we rejoice in Christ, we preach of Christ, we prophesy of Christ, and we write according to our prophecies, that our children may know to what source they may look for a remission of their sins" (2 Nephi 25:26).

It is my humble prayer that He may bless each of us to know what God wants us to teach the rising generation, both inside the temple and outside the temple, so they can be better prepared to make covenants with God, so they can be "armed with righteousness and with the power of God in great glory" (1 Nephi

14:14), so they can withstand the pressures of the world, and so they can perpetuate righteousness for generations to come.

I know that the preaching of the word of God has a great tendency to lead people to do what is just and it has more powerful effect upon the minds than the sword (see Alma 31:5).

The truths of the gospel and the knowledge we receive in the temple prepare us to return to the presence of our Heavenly Father. As we are true to the covenants we make in the house of the Lord, we will have a better understanding of Him, of our Savior Jesus Christ, and of His divine and redeeming mission; we will have the constant companionship of the Holy Ghost; and the power of godliness will be manifested unto us (see D&C 84:20–21).

WE CAN REACH FOR THE SAVIOR WHEN
WE TEACH THE RISING GENERATION
TO CHERISH THE GOSPEL AND THE
BLESSINGS OF THE TEMPLE.

NOTES

1. Mosiah 26:1; Alma 5:49; 3 Nephi 1:30; Doctrine and Covenants 69:8, 123:11; see also Doctrine and Covenants 69:8.

2. Michaelene P. Grassli, "Behold Your Little Ones," *Ensign*, Nov. 1992, 93–94; emphasis added.

3. David A. Bednar, "The Hearts of the Children Shall Turn," *Ensign*, Nov. 2011, 26–27.

4. Thomas S. Monson, "Welcome to Conference," *Ensign*, Nov. 2012, 4–5.

5. See First Presidency Letter, Dec. 14, 2017, https://www.ChurchofJesus Christ.org/bc/content/ldsorg/church/news/2017/12/14/15223_000_letter .pdf?lang=eng.

6. See "Women can serve as witnesses for baptisms, temple sealings, President Nelson announces in historic policy change," *Church News*, https://www .thechurchnews.com/members/2019-10-02/women-can-serve-as-witnesses -for-baptisms-temple-sealings-first-presidency-announces-in-historic-policy -change-162319.

7. Russell M. Nelson, "Ministering," *Ensign*, May 2018, 100.

8. Russell M. Nelson, "Hope of Israel" (worldwide youth devotional, June 3, 2018), HopeofIsrael.ChurchofJesusChrist.org.

9. See Sarah Jane Weaver, "Elder Cook Says Studying Church History Will Deepen Faith during Face to Face Broadcast," *Church News*, Sept. 10, 2018, news.ChurchofJesusChrist.org.

10. Russell M. Nelson, *Teachings of Russell M. Nelson* (Salt Lake City: Deseret Book, 2018), 364.

THAT WE MAY
ALL SIT DOWN IN
HEAVEN TOGETHER

Our two youngest children left on missions at about the same time. It was hard for me and my husband Carlos to adapt to our new life without our children at home. We had to redefine our daily routines and reinvent the way we studied the gospel, bought our food, cooked, and entertained ourselves.

It was during that period of adjustment that I received a new companion for what was then called visiting teaching. When I first saw her name, I thought: "This is going to be interesting!" If anyone were to look at us, it might have looked like we did not have much in common. At that time, she was a newlywed, she was much younger than me, and she was very blonde!

Nevertheless, we started visiting the sisters that were assigned to us. Even though my companion had two jobs and attended school full-time, she made our visits a priority, and we were always able to work around her schedule and minister to our sisters.

It did not take us long to realize that we had a lot in common. For example, she had served a Spanish-speaking mission in California and she loved Mexican food. For a few months we would meet at my house with one of the sisters we visited, and we would cook different Mexican dishes.

This wonderful sister filled the void that my daughter had left, and we became friends. From her, I have learned about resilience, faith, and how to live the gospel more joyfully.

For some reason, there is a notion in the Church that we all must fit a specific mold and that all of our paths have to be the same. We tend to compare ourselves with others, and many of us feel as outsiders to the Church because we do not fit that imaginary mold. The truth is that each of us is unique by divine design and can bring something to the table. When we take the time to get to know other people, we realize that each of us has our own unique story and that we all have had struggles. However, some of us choose not to tell our whole story because it may be too painful.

As we follow the Savior's example of love and compassion toward every person He met, and as we try to love others like He loves us, many painful and unnecessary barriers will come down.

Sometimes we may feel that we do not have anything in common with other fellow Saints. Occasionally, I hear women say, "They assigned me to minister with someone I have nothing in common with, so it will not work out." I want to recommend that the higher, holier way of ministering is to make us feel comfortable sitting down with each other, even if we think we are quite different. We can sometimes be hard on each other as women; we might start judging, comparing, and competing, rather than having compassion and charity. But we can change that culture in the Church, and we must.

It truly does not matter who has ten children and who has none, who is a scientist and who has a third-grade education, or who wears pants and who wears a skirt. To those who say we do not have anything in common, I would suggest that those superficial things matter the least. What unites us is our divine heritage, the people who help us grow spiritually, the assignments we receive from the Lord, our faith in God's plan, our love of Jesus Christ, and our sisterhood in Heavenly Father's family.

I promise you that as we learn to cherish those to whom we minister and with whom we minister, we will be blessed with eternal friendships.

Ministering isn't so much what you do, but what you feel, and how that person feels. Elder Jeffrey R. Holland shared an example. A young mother of five collapsed suddenly. Her husband instinctively called his home teacher. This good brother and his wife immediately ran to the home. The wife stayed with the children while the home teacher drove with the young husband to the hospital. Tragically, the mother did not survive. Elder Holland says that the home teacher stayed with the distressed husband and wept with him—for a long time.[1]

One of the main points of this story was not that the home teacher came at the spur of the moment, but rather that the first instinct the father had was to call his home teacher. The purpose of ministering is not necessarily for us to do something for that person every month, but instead for us to do whatever it takes so that person knows that we are a true friend, and that we will come when they need our help.

This beautiful story shows that ministering does not always have to be a huge act of service. Here is a recent example from my own life. As you can imagine, I was nervous getting ready to give my first talk in general conference. It is a scary assignment! Five-year-old Seth saw me in the hall at Church and said, "I know who is speaking in conference."

"Who?" I asked.

He answered, "You! And I am praying for you, Sister Aburto." A five-year-old ministered to me. I felt so loved. It does not require much for a person to feel loved. I add my witness that offering comfort is one of the most Christlike acts we can perform for others.

I know we are all making our best effort. As President Henry B. Eyring said at the April 2017 general conference: "My purpose today is both to reassure you and invigorate you. . . . Perhaps you have come to this [conference] wondering whether your service has been acceptable. And at the same time, you may sense that there is more to do—perhaps much more!"[2]

President Russell M. Nelson has said: "Ministering is caring for

Lord's way. . . . Ministering is part of our own process
e as we turn our hearts to God and His children. And
, those to whom we minister are drawn closer to the
ir own efforts to repent. . . . As we embrace the gift of
repentance we will rise up and minister in a holier way."³

Repenting and ministering go hand in hand with our efforts
to fulfill the two greatest commandments: to love God and to love
our neighbor as Jesus Christ loves us. When we repent, we get
closer to Heavenly Father and the Savior, and our love for Them
grows. When we minister, we get closer to our neighbor—which
includes our family, our co-servants in the gospel, and even strangers—and our love for them grows. In addition to increasing our
love for God when we repent, our love for others grows, and when
we minister to others, our love for God grows.

I would like to illustrate this principle with an example from
my own life. When I joined the Church, I was twenty-six years old
and had just gone through a divorce. I had a son, and finances were
tight. When the missionaries explained the law of tithing to me, I
wanted to contribute, but it seemed impossible for me to obey that
commandment. Every time I received a paycheck, I had a pile of
bills to pay and I barely had any money left. Because of that reality,
I did not pay a full tithing; I just paid the little that I had left at the
end of the month, and I went on like that for a few years.

One evening, I was with a group of friends. We were just visiting with each other. For some reason, we started talking about
money, and I felt impressed to open up to them. So, I told them,

"I have the desire to pay a full tithing, but I just can't do it." They listened to me intently and lovingly, and suddenly, the room was filled with the Spirit.

One by one, my dear friends testified to me about the law of tithing. One of them said, "Reyna, you need to prove the Lord so He can open the windows of heaven and pour blessings on you and your family" (see Malachi 3:10).

Another one told me, "If you ask the Lord for help, He will help you. Remember His promise when He said, 'Ask, and it shall be given you; seek, and ye shall find; knock, and it shall be opened unto you'" (Matthew 7:7).

A third one counseled me, "Maybe you could follow a different approach. Try paying your tithing as soon as you get a paycheck, even if it is every week. Pay your tithing first, and you will see how everything else will fall into place."

In the end, we were all crying, and we felt we were standing in a holy place. My friends did not judge me, they did not point fingers at me, and they were not self-righteous. They had a sincere concern for me, and they genuinely wanted to help. They strengthened me, they called me to repentance, and they gently invited me to come unto Christ. They exemplified what it looks like to have pure, Christlike love.

That night, I knelt by my bed, poured my heart out to my Heavenly Father, and pleaded for help. I felt the sweet assurance that if I made a sincere effort, He would help me. Then I decided that I would follow my friends' counsel.

At the end of the month, a miracle happened: I was able to pay my tithing and all my other obligations. I did not have any money left, I did not get any extra money, but I was able to obey the law of tithing, and that was a miracle! Month after month, it was a recurring miracle that filled me with joy and gratitude.

Several months after that, another great blessing and another miracle came into my life. I started dating my husband Carlos, and we were able to be sealed in the temple because I was paying my tithing. The windows of heaven had truly opened for me.

We should not underestimate the influence that we may have on our friends whenever we share our testimony with them and whenever we try to strengthen them in the Lord (see Alma 15:18). That conversation with my friends in which they manifested their love for God and for me was a turning point in my life with eternal consequences and blessings. They ministered to me in a way that helped me draw closer to God and repent.

I know that the Lord accepts all our efforts. The invitation from our prophet to minister to each other in new and holier ways is not necessarily asking us to do more—our lists are already very full! But maybe we can do the right things. The simple things. The things the Lord Himself wants done.

I learned this principle some years ago. When I was working full-time out of the home, I used to make long lists of things that needed to be done on Saturday. I could never finish everything on my list. A major milestone happened when I realized I did not need a long list for Saturday. I started to save my Saturdays for more important family time by going shopping or doing laundry on weeknights, so I would be free. My advice from my own experience is to just pick two or three things on the "to-do" list that are realistic and let the other stuff go. Spend time having fun! Enjoy your family! Work together! Allow them to help with what needs to be done! Do uplifting things with them!

Years after that realization, I started working at home. I thought: Now I am going to have more time. I do not have meetings. I do not have to drive to work or make a lunch to take. But I soon learned that my assumptions were not correct. Even though I tried to be disciplined in turning my computer on at eight and turning it off at five, I felt that I was never done! I felt that I would never get where I wanted to be by the end of each day.

One day, I realized I will never be done. My lists will never be finished. It is not possible. I want to tell everyone what I have learned. You do not have to do it all, and you are never done, and you can be okay with that, and you can accept that. Do what you can each day, ask the Lord to fill in the gaps, and then, a new day starts, and you begin again. That is part of the beauty of being disciples of Jesus Christ, that we are never done, that there is always something else to do, and that there is always room for improvement.

I testify that we are daughters and sons of heavenly parents and, as such, each of us has a divine nature and destiny.

I testify that our Father in Heaven loves us, and that He is mindful of us. He knows our heart and He is willing to bless us so we can return to His presence.

I know that as we make an effort to minister to each other in a newer, higher and holier way, we will be led by the Spirit and the Lord will take us by the hand. He will be our light and He will prepare the way before us. He will open our eyes and our ears, He will magnify our abilities, and He will help us become what He has prepared us to become.

Let us cherish one another, watch over one another, comfort one another, and gain instruction, so we can strengthen each other in the Lord, and so we can sit down in heaven together, where the Lord will lead us unto living fountains of waters and He will wipe away all tears from our eyes.

May we do all of this with the love for God and the love for each other in our heart, as we follow the promptings of the Spirit.

WE CAN REACH FOR THE SAVIOR AS
WE MINISTER TO OTHERS WITH LOVE
AND ACCEPTANCE IN OUR HEARTS.

NOTES

1. See Jeffrey R. Holland, "Be With and Strengthen Them," *Ensign*, May 2018, 102–3.

2. Henry B. Eyring, "Walk with Me," *Ensign*, May 2017, 82.

3. Russell M. Nelson, General Conference Leadership Meeting, Apr. 2019.

TIMES OF TRIAL

While I was growing up, my life was not easy. By the time my youngest brother, Henry, was born in 1975, things were always tense at home. My parents would fight all the time, and sometimes they did not speak to each other for weeks. My father was an alcoholic. He would drink mostly on weekends, but sometimes even during the week. It was like he had two different personalities, one when he was sober and one when he was drunk.

Yet my father was always nice to me. I knew he loved me by the way he treated me, but many times I would feel anger toward him because he was mean to my mother when he was drunk. I felt that our life would have been so different if he did not have that weakness.

In 1978, there was a lot of tension in Nicaragua. The only

conversation topic for everyone was the civil unrest taking place in different cities. We were all afraid that, sooner or later, a civil war would break out in Managua.

At the end of June 1979, it finally happened. The rebels took over part of the city. They were in control of several neighborhoods on the east side of Managua. Little by little they moved closer to our neighborhood. Bombs and gunfire were set off in the distance. They sounded louder at night.

The city of Managua was practically paralyzed. The schools, the government offices, and many businesses were closed. There was movement on the west side of the city, but life was not normal for anyone. The air was heavy, and we all felt uncertain about the future.

At home, we put our mattresses on the floor and slept there, hoping that we would be protected in case the bullets made it into our home. We had been eating the small reserve that we had. One by one, the chickens from our backyard became part of our food. We did not have a lot to eat, but we had enough. The neighbors helped each other. Someone would share a big sack of sugar, another one a big sack of flour, and we all got by. We also sat together in big groups and the adults would tell stories. There was a special feeling of unity between all of us amidst all the turmoil and the danger around us. It felt like we all belonged to a big family, as the kindness of people was evident in small acts of love.

The government had control over all forms of public communication. At night, we would listen to radio stations from Costa

Rica because the Nicaraguan stations had been shut down. We would hear how the government was trying to make the rebels leave the city and about all the atrocities that were happening.

After a couple of weeks, the military tried bombarding from the air the parts of the city taken by the rebels. Every afternoon, around four o'clock, we would see planes flying over the east part of the city. We saw them shooting bullets. We also saw helicopters throwing big barrels of explosives.

On the radio, we would hear the reports of the damage caused every day by those bombs. Houses were being destroyed. Entire families were being killed. It was hard for me to watch those planes and helicopters every afternoon, knowing that every bomb they dropped was killing lots of people, including children. However, it was also hard *not* to watch. All the neighbors would come out to the street to watch the planes and helicopters. It was scary to see them turning in our direction as they would circle around their targets.

As I watched all that madness, destruction, and injustice, I would ask myself, *Why does God allow this to happen? Why doesn't He do something to stop it?* I was not upset with God, but I had those questions in my heart.

Many years later, I learned that one of the most precious gifts we have received from God is our agency, which is our ability to choose our actions. The Book of Mormon teaches, "Wherefore, men . . . are free to choose liberty and eternal life, through the great Mediator of all men, or to choose captivity and death"

(2 Nephi 2:27). Agency is an eternal principle that we exercised in the premortal life, where we learned about Heavenly Father's plan of salvation and had the opportunity to choose for ourselves if we wanted to follow Him and His plan.

Fortunately, something happened in Nicaragua and the situation was resolved as the president left the country. I remember vividly that day after he left, when the rebels were celebrating their victory out in the streets. I think I have never lived another day like that—in which everyone was extremely happy, feeling collective joy and thinking that our problems were over.

After graduating from high school, I started attending college. I always enjoyed learning and getting an education. However, over the years, the situation in Nicaragua was just getting worse. I decided to marry a young man that I was dating, and we left the country shortly after. We arrived in San Francisco in October 1984.

My first months in the United States were hard because that first winter felt very cold, coming from a warm climate. I also had to get used to a new culture and a new language, and my family was still in Nicaragua. However, I was extremely grateful to be in this magnificent country. I felt greatly blessed because I had a job that paid $3.35 an hour and a place to live. I had the desire and means to help my family move in with me. After some time, my mother and two siblings arrived in San Francisco.

I would attend school at night, first to an English-as-a-second-language school and then to the City College of San Francisco. My son Xavier was born two years later. He brought immense joy for me and my family. He was a healthy and sharp little boy who gave me a beautiful reason to keep going and to try harder.

However, my husband drank alcohol and used drugs. Over time, his addictions worsened. He stopped working and sometimes he would be gone for days. The situation had become unbearable for me. I started attending Alcoholics Anonymous meetings and seeing a therapist to find out how I could help him. I learned that I also needed help.

After a series of events that clearly showed me that both my three-year-old son and I were in danger, I took the painful and yet liberating decision to permanently separate from my husband and get a divorce. Even after he was gone, I still did not feel at peace. What if he came back? How would I raise my son so he could be a good boy and become a good man? Where would I find solace for my soul? How would our future be?

I know that sometimes things happen in our life over which we do not have control. Other people make decisions that may hurt us. We have longings, we have questions, things happen to us that do not seem to have a reason. But if we listen to the Lord, He will "speak peace to our souls . . . [and] cause us that we should hope for our deliverance in him" (Alma 58:11). If we are patient, if we put our trust on our Savior, if we wait on His timing, and we try to follow His commandments, answers will come one day, and we will finally have that peace that we are looking for.

Elder Dieter F. Uchtdorf once told the story of a magnificent

Lutheran church in Dresden, Germany, which was destroyed during World War II. Years later, the church was rebuilt using many of the original bricks that were burnt during the bombing, and that is why some of the bricks are black.

I feel that my life is like that church. I have gone through hard times. The scars, the consequences, and the pain are still there. However, the Lord Jesus Christ has rebuilt my life and has allowed me to have joy through His tender mercies and through the enabling power of His Atonement. I know that He is our Savior and our Redeemer, that He is the source of peace and healing. I have felt "encircled . . . in the arms of his love" (2 Nephi 1:15). He is always extending His arms of mercy and love toward us so we can turn to Him and have a better life as well as eternal life.

Like Elder Uchtdorf said referring to that church in Germany: "If man can take the ruins, rubble, and remains of a broken city and rebuild an awe-inspiring structure that rises toward the heavens, how much more capable is our Almighty Father to restore His children who have fallen, struggled, or become lost?

"It matters not how completely ruined our lives may seem. It matters not how scarlet our sins, how deep our bitterness, how lonely, abandoned, or broken our hearts may be. Even those who are without hope, who live in despair, who have betrayed trust, surrendered their integrity, or turned away from God can be rebuilt. Save those rare sons of perdition, there is no life so shattered that it cannot be restored.

"The joyous news of the gospel is this: because of the eternal plan of happiness provided by our loving Heavenly Father and through the infinite sacrifice of Jesus the Christ, we can not only be redeemed from our fallen state and restored to purity, but we can also transcend mortal imagination and become heirs of eternal life and partakers of God's indescribable glory."[1]

We all go through hard times, we all have tribulation in our life, we are all in need of healing, and we are all in need of redeeming grace. Part of our mortal existence is to go through trials, big and small, at different times of our life, but Heavenly Father will "consecrate [our] afflictions for [our] gain" (2 Nephi 2:2). Those tough times make us stronger and allow us to be sensitive to others. I am grateful for the hardships I have gone through because they have shaped me, have allowed me to know what I know, and have given me humility to acknowledge my dependency on my Heavenly Father and my Lord Jesus Christ. They have also given me a chance to feel Their love and concern for me, individually. I know that our Heavenly Father and our Savior are mindful of each of us.

If you are going through a hard time in your life, please do not give up, please keep trying, please keep reaching to the Savior so He can heal you. I know that we can all be healed by the soothing balm that our Master Healer, Jesus Christ, offers us in His infinite and perfect love.

I know that Jesus Christ will one day come back to this earth "clothed with power and great glory" (D&C 45:44). At that time, His trump will sound, and every ear will hear it, every knee will bow, and every tongue will confess before Him (see D&C 88:104; Mosiah 27:31). We will then rejoice collectively, with everlasting joy.

WE CAN REACH FOR THE SAVIOR BY PATIENTLY AWAITING THE ANSWERS AND BLESSINGS WE SEEK, EVEN AMID TRIALS.

NOTES

1. Dieter F. Uchtdorf, "He Will Place You on His Shoulders and Carry You Home," *Ensign*, May 2016, 101–2.

THE LORD SHALL BE OUR EVERLASTING LIGHT

As part of our mortal experience, we all go through times of darkness and light; episodes of sadness and joy; moments of despair and hope; lapses of uneasiness and peace; and periods of weakness and strength. In the scriptures we read that to have joy, we have to know misery (see 2 Nephi 2:23), and that there has to be "opposition in all things" (2 Nephi 2:11). Illnesses of the brain are part of that opposition we face in the flesh.

In my personal case, although I have gone through what some call "situational sadness"[1] as I have faced challenges in my life, I can say that, up to this point, I have not experienced clinical depression.

My first conscious experience with that kind of trial came as I saw my daughter Elena suffer from the ailment of depression during her late teenage years. It took her and me years to realize that she was afflicted with depression and social anxiety. When she finally understood that she needed help, our journey to her healing began. Like every other journey, ours included pleading for divine help, pouring our hearts to our Maker to solicit His guidance, and trusting in His power to take us by the hand. As I look back, I realize that the answers from our Heavenly Father came little by little, and in subtle ways. However, it required our faith to take one step at a time.

After she graduated from high school, it was hard for Elena to keep a job because of her social anxiety. She started college and thrived there because tasks such as taking classes, fulfilling school assignments, and taking tests are things that can be done in isolation. It was during that time that she felt through the Spirit that she needed to serve a mission. In preparation for that, she realized that she needed professional help to address her depression and anxiety. She also got a new job and she was adamant about keeping it, which she did until she left on her mission.

I felt that my role at that time was to be her listening partner. When she came home late in the evening after work, we would sit at our dining table and have long conversations. She would tell me about her struggles at school and work, and I would listen to her, cry with her, hug her, give her words of comfort, and pray with her.

After receiving therapy for some time, she felt better and left on her mission, where she found many angels that helped her through it. Her mission president and his wife, her mission companions, the other sisters and elders serving in the Modesto California Mission, Church members, friends whom she taught, relatives and friends back home who cheered her on remotely, all of them, knowingly and unknowingly, became instruments in the hand of God to give her comfort and strength.

She then hit a valley about halfway through her mission. When reading her messages, I knew that she was not doing well, and it was hard for me not to be able to be by her side helping her. One Sunday night, I could not sleep because I felt a heavy weight on my heart. I got up, went to another room, and wept for a long time. After I let out my emotions, I knelt and pleaded to my Father in Heaven to let me know what I could do. I eventually felt peace in my heart, went back to bed and, after a while, fell asleep aided by the exhaustion I felt.

When I woke up the next morning, a clear thought came to my mind: *I do not know anything about depression; I need to learn about it so I can help my daughter.* That simple prompting was the answer I was longing for. From that day on, I searched for information about depression and anxiety in different Church resources.

I printed many of the articles and materials that I found, sent copies to Elena, and asked her to study them and to share them with others in her mission. I told her that I would do the same. I also suggested to her to look for professional help through her mission president. She did, he made the arrangements, and a counselor helped her with a few sessions, which made a big difference and allowed her to continue to serve the Lord Jesus Christ by preaching His gospel and to feel the joy of helping others come to Him.

The more I read, studied, and pondered, the more I realized that emotional ailments are more common than we think, and that unknowingly, society and traditions may make them worse. One of the most astonishing discoveries I made was that perfectionism is one of the main causes of depression and anxiety. I always thought that trying to do things perfectly was a good and desirable trait. I learned that in some measure it is, because we need to keep stretching ourselves and trying to do our best in all we do. However, when we take it to an extreme and we do not allow ourselves and others to realize that as human beings we have limitations, then it becomes damaging and debilitating. Understanding and knowing with every cell of our body that we will always fall short in everything we do and that we need the grace of Jesus Christ to carry us all along is one of the most empowering and enlightening truths that we can embrace.

Elena finished her mission at the end of March 2017, just three days before I was sustained in my calling as the Second Counselor in the Relief Society General Presidency of The Church of Jesus Christ of Latter-day Saints. Little did I know at that time that the journey she and I went through together was going to be part of the preparation I had been given by my Father in Heaven to fulfill my calling.

As I visited small and big gatherings of people as part of that calling in different parts of the world; as I had conversations with individuals, families, leaders, missionaries, and my own relatives; as I read letters sent to our presidency; as I searched the scriptures looking for revelation and strength; as I fasted and prayed pleading for divine guidance; as I constantly looked for ways to fulfill my calling the best I could; and as I tried to apply the atoning grace of Jesus Christ and the redeeming power of His Atonement in all that I did, I realized that each of us are in great and constant need of His empowering and liberating healing.

Over and over, I would get the feeling that the subject of emotional issues needed to be addressed more openly among the members of our Church. When I received my first assignment to speak in general conference, it was one of the topics that came to my mind and heart as I pondered what the Lord wanted me to say. At that point, I realized that the topic of emotional stress required a lot of preparation and time from my part, and I did not have much of the latter at that point. As I kept pondering, the Spirit guided me in another direction in that first assignment. However, I started recording ideas and thoughts about emotional illness as they came to my mind and heart.

I know that there are many other forms of mental and emotional afflictions that exist, but for the sake of simplicity, I mostly mention depression and anxiety in this text.

When I received my second assignment to speak in the sacred venue of general conference, I started the divine process of pleading for heavenly guidance to know the direction I needed to go. I prayed, fasted, pondered, and listened. Interestingly, during those days, I had conversations with people who brought up the topic of depression and anxiety without me giving them any hints that it was in my mind and heart. I then looked over my notes on the subject and with them in my hands, I asked Heavenly Father, *Is this what You want me to speak about?* As other promptings came, I started going in that direction, knowing that if it was not the right thing to do, the Spirit would let me know.

As I started the process of writing my talk, the image of the experience I'd had years before flying on a plane as it approached a severe storm at the end of the day kept coming to my mind. On that day, when we were above the heavy clouds, we could not visualize the darkness that lay just a few feet below us, and when we were enveloped in the darkness underneath as we descended, it was difficult to visualize the radiance of the sun that shone just a few feet above us. That image had made such an impression on me that every time I read or thought about how people feel when they suffer from a brain illness, it reminded me of those dark clouds I saw and how they blocked the intense light coming from the sun above them. Similarly, as I learned how hard it can be for people who do not suffer those illnesses to believe that they are real, it reminded me of how the sun hitting on those same clouds made them so bright that it was hard to imagine the darkness underneath them.

It was the perfect image to hopefully help people realize that when someone's brain is suffering, the problem is the illness, or the cloud, and not the person herself or himself. It is not his or her fault. There is no need to find out whose fault it is. What that person needs is to receive healing from our Savior Jesus Christ and to understand that they do not have to suffer through it alone.

One of the sad consequences of those black clouds that may form in our lives is that they can blind us to God's light and even cause us to question if that light exists for us anymore. Heavenly Father and His Son Jesus Christ are always close to us, ready to help us when we turn to Them, but those clouds may block us from feeling Their love.

Another sad reality about these ailments is that they can distort the way we perceive ourselves, others, and even God. I feel that they are the cause of many problems in the world, like abuse, divorce, addictions, and even war. They are universal and affect women and men of all ages, of all walks of life, everywhere.

Likewise damaging is the desensitizing cloud of skepticism and judgment that can affect those who have not experienced these challenges. Many of us grew up thinking that if we have enough faith, all problems can be solved. Faith is a powerful source of healing, especially if it is centered in Jesus Christ and in His ability to heal us. However, our faith also needs to include the actions necessary to receive that healing, because we "*are justified* of faith *and works, through* grace" (Joseph Smith Translation, Romans 4:16; see also James 2:17; 1 Nephi 16:28).

During His mortal ministry, Jesus Christ healed the sick and the afflicted, but each person had to exercise faith in Him and act to receive His healing. Some walked for long distances, others extended their hand to touch His garment, and others had to be carried to Him to be healed.[2]

It is important for us to learn and know how our body functions and that we are in a mortal state in which we unavoidably experience the realities of the flesh. Our brain, like other parts of our body, is subject to illnesses, trauma, and chemical imbalances.

I once heard someone say that when we study the human body, we are studying God, since we were made in His image. The Proclamation on the Family states: "All human beings—male and female—are created in the image of God. Each is a beloved spirit son or daughter of heavenly parents, and, as such, each has a divine nature and destiny."[3] Like our heavenly parents and our Savior, we have a physical body, and within that body,[4] we have a spirit and experience emotions.[5] Our emotions are part of that divine nature that we have inherited from Them. Knowing this can help us as we learn to cope with our emotions in healthy ways, to address brain illnesses and to find sources of healing from the damage that they cause. Learning to identify and value our emotions can help us use them constructively to become more like our Savior, Jesus Christ.

It is normal to feel sad or worried occasionally. Sadness and anxiety are natural human emotions[6] that occur when things have not turned out the way we have expected, when events change the course of our life, when others hurt us or someone else either intentionally or unintentionally, when we have made mistakes, or for other reasons out of our control. There is nothing to be ashamed of with letting ourselves cry, with expressing our feelings, and with working through our emotions. In fact, through the process of crying, we let out the pressure that is inside us, we liberate ourselves of burdens and fears, and somehow, we clean and wash our eyes so we can see more clearly and with an eternal perspective.

However, if we are constantly sad and if our pain blocks our ability to feel the love of our Heavenly Father and His Son and the influence of the Holy Ghost, then we may need to realize that we are beyond sadness and that we may be suffering from depression, anxiety, or another emotional condition. When our minds are suffering, it is appropriate to seek help from God, from those around us, and from medical and mental health professionals. Acknowledging that we need help is the first step toward feeling the Spirit in our life again.

Elena described her darkest moments this way: "One of the hardest trials I ever had to endure was sadness. There was a time in my life when I was extremely sad all the time. I always thought that sadness was something to be ashamed of, and that it was a sign of weakness. So, I kept my sadness to myself."[7]

My friend Naomi described it this way: "Since my early childhood, I have faced a constant battle with feelings of hopelessness, darkness, loneliness, and fear and the sense that I am broken or defective. I did everything to hide my pain and to never give the impression that I was anything but thriving and strong."[8]

Unfortunately, there are so many of us who feel this way—too many of us that constantly feel surrounded by a suffocating and numbing darkness that does not allow us to see or feel any divine goodness around us, and so many of us who suffer in silence, solitude, and isolation because we do not know how and where to ask for help.

The reality is that it can happen to any of us—especially when, as believers in the plan of happiness, we place unnecessary burdens on ourselves by thinking we need to be perfect now. Such thoughts can be overwhelming and debilitating. Achieving perfection is a process that will take place throughout our mortal life and beyond—and only through the grace of Jesus Christ.[9]

In contrast, when we are open about our emotional challenges, admitting we are not perfect, we give others permission to share their struggles. Together we realize there is hope and we do not have to suffer alone. We need to open the dialogue and talk about these issues in appropriate ways with our children, families, and friends in our homes, wards, and communities.

Our Father in Heaven designed our mortal experience to be one in which we would need to rely not only on the Savior but also upon one another to successfully complete our journey back to our heavenly home. As disciples of Jesus Christ, we have made a covenant with God that we "are willing to bear one another's burdens, that they may be light" and "to mourn with those that mourn; yea, and comfort those that stand in need of comfort" (Mosiah 18:8–9). Our Savior has also asked us to feed His lambs and His sheep.[10] Doing all of this may include becoming informed about emotional illnesses, finding resources that can help address these struggles, and ultimately bringing ourselves and others to Christ, who is the Master Healer, so He can heal us.[11]

Many times, we do not know what to say or how to react because we cannot visualize what the other person is going through. However, informing ourselves about the reality and prevalence of emotional issues allows us to feel and show more compassion for the pain that others are enduring. Even if we do not know how to relate to what others are going through, validating that their pain is real can be an important first step in finding understanding and healing. Knowing how to recognize signs and symptoms in ourselves and others can be helpful. We can also learn to detect inaccurate or unhealthy thinking patterns and how to replace them with more accurate and healthier ones.[12]

In some cases, the cause of depression or anxiety can be identified, while other times it may be harder to discern. Depression can also result from positive life changes—such as the birth of a child or a new job—and can occur when things are good in a person's life. Our brains may suffer because of stress,[13] perfectionism, fear of judgment, sorrow for sin, fear for the future, or staggering fatigue.[14] It can sometimes be improved through adjustments in diet, sleep, and exercise, talking about our emotions with our Heavenly Father in our prayers and in our conversations with others, turning outward instead of inward,[15] and drawing upon the divine grace that Jesus Christ offers us. Other times therapy or medication under the direction of trained professionals may also be needed.

Elder Richard G. Scott once said: "The beginning of healing

requires childlike faith in the unalterable fact that Father in Heaven loves you and has supplied a way to heal. His Beloved Son, Jesus Christ, laid down His life to provide that healing. But there is no magic solution, no simple balm to provide healing, nor is there an easy path to the complete remedy. The cure requires profound faith in Jesus Christ and in His infinite capacity to heal."[16]

Untreated mental or emotional illness can lead to increased isolation, misunderstandings, broken relationships, self-harm, and even suicide. I know this firsthand, as my own father died by suicide many years ago. His death was shocking and heartbreaking for my family and me. At the time, he was living in San Francisco, California, and we did not know that he was suffering emotionally. We never imagined that he would do something like that. Even now, it is something that I still cannot grasp or explain.

It has taken me years to work through my grief. For a long time, I did not want to talk about it, because it was too painful. I was afraid that if I told my children, they could get suicidal ideas. Now I know that I was wrong and that talking about suicide in appropriate ways actually helps to prevent it rather than encourage it.[17] As I was preparing my general conference talk about these topics, I realized that I could not be a hypocrite. I could not tell people to be open about their struggles if I was not willing to do the same. Thus, I finally openly discussed my father's death with my children.

Although talking about it was difficult, it was also relieving for me. Now I know that part of the healing process is to be able to talk about our pain, to let others cry with us, and to allow the Savior to work His miracles on us. I have certainly witnessed the healing that He can give on both sides of the veil. I am looking forward to meeting my father on the other side of the veil one day, so I can tell him how much I love him and to ask him for forgiveness for not being by his side when he needed me the most.

Sadly, many members of our Church who suffer from severe depression distance themselves from their fellow Saints because they feel they do not fit some imaginary idea of what they think their life should look like. For some reason, there is this notion of a mold in which we all fit or should fit. The truth is that each of us is different and has a different story. When we introduce ourselves to others, we say the things that we think they want to hear and we leave things out, because they are too personal or too painful to air publicly. This means that every person we meet, even someone who seems to be happy or is indeed happy, carries some pain in her or his heart. The truth is that we are all healing from something and are all in need of healing.

We can help those who may feel that they do not fit in know that they do indeed belong with us. It is important to recognize that depression is not the result of weakness, nor is it usually the result of sin (see John 9:1–7). It "thrives in secrecy but shrinks in empathy."[18] Together, we can break through the clouds of isolation and stigma so the burden of shame is lifted, and miracles of healing can occur.

We can follow the Savior's path and increase our compassion, diminish our tendency to judge, and stop being the inspectors of the spirituality of others. We are all making our best effort to follow God's commandments. "Let us not therefore judge one another any more" (Romans 14:13). Listening with love is one of the greatest gifts we can offer, and we may be able to help carry or lift the heavy clouds that suffocate our loved ones and friends (see Romans 2:19; 13:12) so that, through our love, they can once again feel the Holy Ghost and perceive the light that emanates from Jesus Christ, "a light which cannot be hid in darkness" (D&C 14:9). When it comes to healing, don't we all need Him desperately? "Are we not all beggars?" (Mosiah 4:19).[19]

When there is a problem, our tendency is to fix it. However, we do not have to become sole fixers of ourselves or of others. We do not have to do everything ourselves. On more than one occasion in my life, I have sought therapists to help me deal with difficult times. There are times in our lives when we must give comfort, and other times when we must be willing to receive it at the hands of others. No matter how weak we feel, there is always something that we can do to bring hope to someone.

If you are constantly surrounded by a "mist of darkness" (1 Nephi 8:23–24), I plea to you to turn to Heavenly Father. Nothing that you have experienced can change the eternal truth that you are His child and that He loves you.[20] Remember that Christ is your Savior and Redeemer, and God is your Father. They understand. Picture Them close by you, listening and offering support.[21] "[They] will console you in your afflictions" (Jacob 3:1).

Read your patriarchal blessing or ask for a priesthood blessing so you can hear and remember how much Heavenly Father loves you and wants to bless you. Do all you can and trust in the Lord's atoning grace.

Your struggles do not define you, but they can *refine* you.[22] Because of a "thorn in the flesh" (2 Corinthians 12:7), you may have the ability to feel more compassion toward others and to "be filled with love towards God and all men [and women]" (Mosiah 2:4). As guided by the Holy Spirit, share your story in order to "succor the weak, lift up the hands which hang down, and strengthen the feeble knees" (D&C 81:5; see also Isaiah 35:3). Seek opportunities to build stronger connections with others.

We can all become healers and helpers. Elder Jeffrey R. Holland extended this invitation: "I ask you to be a healer, be a helper, be someone who joins in the work of Christ in lifting burdens, in making the load lighter, in making things better. Isn't that the phrase we used to use as children when we had a bump or a bruise? Didn't we say to Mom or Dad, 'Make it better.' Well, lots of people on your right hand and on your left are carrying bumps and bruises that they hope will be healed and made whole. Someone . . . within reasonable proximity to you . . . is carrying a spiritual or physical or emotional burden of some sort or some other affliction drawn from life's catalog of a thousand kinds of sorrow."[23]

My daughter Elena has gone a long way in her struggles with depression. After years of seeking healing from our Savior, she wrote: "Looking back, I have noticed blessings that have come from that trial [with emotional issues]. For example, I have learned how to cope with those sad feelings, and I learned how to deal with rejection, . . . and with feelings of embarrassment, among other things. This new knowledge is something that I will use . . . for the rest of my life. This trial has made me stronger. And for that I am so grateful. . . . During this sad time, I felt completely worthless, but that trial gave me the chance to truly exercise my faith in the plan of salvation. For I knew that my Heavenly Father loved me, and that He had a plan just for me, and that Christ understood exactly what I was going through."

My friend Naomi has also found solace for her soul. She shared the following with me: "The healing balm of my Savior's Atonement has been the most constant source of peace and refuge throughout my journey. When I feel alone in my struggle, I am reminded that He has already experienced exactly what I am going through on my behalf. . . . There is so much hope in knowing that my future perfected, resurrected body will not be plagued by this mortal [affliction]."

For those of us currently struggling or supporting someone who is struggling, let us be willing to follow God's commandments so we may always have His Spirit with us (see Moroni 4:3; D&C 20:77). Let us do the "small and simple things" (Alma 37:6) that will give us spiritual strength so we can face our afflictions. As President Russell M. Nelson said: "Nothing opens the heavens quite like the combination of increased purity, exact obedience, earnest seeking, daily feasting on the words of Christ in the Book of Mormon, and regular time committed to temple and family history work."[24]

Let us all remember that our Savior, Jesus Christ, "hath born our griefs and carried our sorrows" (Isaiah 53:4; see also Mosiah 14:4). He "[has taken] upon him [our] infirmities, that his bowels may be filled with mercy, according to the flesh, that he may know . . . how to succor [us] according to [our] infirmities" (Alma 7:12; see also 2 Nephi 9:21). He came "to bind up the brokenhearted, . . . to comfort all that mourn; . . . to give unto them beauty for ashes, the oil of joy for mourning, the garment of praise for the spirit of heaviness" (Isaiah 61:1–3; see also Luke 4:18).

I know that "thru cloud and sunshine"[25] the Lord will abide with us; that our "afflictions [can be] swallowed up in the joy of Christ" (Alma 31:38); that when thick darkness gathers around us, His light shines above the brightness of the sun (see Joseph Smith—History 1:15–16); and that "it is by grace that we are saved, after all we can do" (2 Nephi 25:23). I also know that Jesus Christ will return to the earth "with healing in his wings" (Malachi 4:2; 3 Nephi 25:2). Ultimately, He "shall wipe away all tears from [our] eyes; and there shall be no more . . . sorrow" (Revelation 21:4). For all who will "come unto Christ, and be perfected in him" (Moroni 10:32), the "sun shall no more go down . . . for the Lord shall be [our] everlasting light, and the days of [our] mourning shall be ended" (Isaiah 60:20).

WE CAN REACH FOR THE SAVIOR WHEN
WE TURN TO HIM IN TIMES OF SORROW
AND AFFLICTION, RELYING ON HIS
LIGHT TO SUSTAIN US IN DARKNESS.

NOTES

1. Jane Clayson Johnson, *Silent Souls Weeping* (Salt Lake City: Deseret Book, 2018), 4.
2. See Matthew 9:2–7, 20–22; 14:35–36; Mark 1:40–42; 2:3–5; 3 Nephi 17:6–7.
3. "The Family: A Proclamation to the World," *Ensign*, Nov. 2010, 129.
4. "The spirit and the body are the soul of man" (Doctrine and Covenants 88:15). "Your body is the temple for your spirit. And how you use your body affects your spirit" (Russell M. Nelson, "Decisions for Eternity," *Ensign*, Nov. 2013, 107).
5. See, for example, Isaiah 65:19; Luke 7:13; 3 Nephi 17:6–7; Moses 7:28.
6. See "Sadness and Depression," kidshealth.org/en/kids/depression.html.
7. Hermana Elena Aburto blog, hermanaelenaaburto.blogspot.com/2015/08/. She also wrote: "God does not shame you when you are lacking a skill. He is happy to help you improve and repent. He does not expect you to fix everything at once. You don't have to do this alone" (iwillhealthee.blogspot .com/2018/09/).
8. Personal correspondence.
9. See Russell M. Nelson, "Perfection Pending," *Ensign*, Nov. 1995, 86–88; Jeffrey R. Holland, "Be Ye Therefore Perfect—Eventually," *Ensign*, Nov. 2017, 40–42; Gerrit W. Gong, "Becoming Perfect in Christ," *Ensign*, July 2014, 14–19; J. Devn Cornish, "Am I Good Enough? Will I Make It?" *Ensign*, Nov. 2016, 32–34; Cecil O. Samuelson, "What Does It Mean to Be Perfect?" *New Era*, Jan. 2006, 10–13.
10. See John 21:15–18; see also Russell M. Nelson, "Shepherds, Lambs and Home Teachers," *Ensign*, Aug. 1994, 16.
11. See Russell M. Nelson, "Jesus Christ—the Master Healer," *Ensign*, Nov.

2005, 85–88; Carole M. Stephens, "The Master Healer," *Ensign*, Nov. 2016, 9–12

12. See *Emotional Resilience for Self-Reliance* (2020), https://www.Churchof JesusChrist.org/self-reliance/course-materials/emotional-resilience-self -reliance-course-video-resources.

13. See "Understanding Stress," *Adjusting to Missionary Life* (2013), 5–10.

14. See Jeffrey R. Holland, "Like a Broken Vessel," *Ensign*, Nov. 2013, 40.

15. See David B. Bednar, "The Character of Christ," https://www2.byui.edu /Presentations/Transcripts/ReligionSymposium/2003_01_25_Bednar.htm; see also https://www.thechurchnews.com/leaders-and-ministry/2019-07-09 /elder-bednar-character-christ-2019-mission-leadership-seminar-50286.

16. Richard G. Scott, "To Heal the Shattering Consequences of Abuse," *Ensign*, May 2008, 42.

17. See Dale G. Renlund, "Understanding Suicide" (video), ChurchofJesus Christ.org/study/manual/videos/understanding-suicide, and "Talking about Suicide" (video), ChurchofJesusChrist.org/study/manual/videos/talking -about-suicide; Kenishi Shimokawa, "Understanding Suicide: Warning Signs and Prevention," *Ensign*, Oct. 2016, 34–39.

18. *Silent Souls Weeping*, 197

19. See Jeffrey R. Holland, "Are We Not All Beggars?" *Ensign*, Nov. 2014, 40–42.

20. See Psalm 82:6; Romans 8:16–18; Doctrine and Covenants 24:1; 76:24; Moses 1:1–39.

21. See *Adjusting to Missionary Life,* 20; see also Micah 7:8; Matthew 4:16; Luke 1:78–79; John 8:12.

22. See 2 Corinthians 4:16–18; Doctrine and Covenants 121:7–8, 33; 122:5–9.

23. Jeffrey R. Holland, "Come unto Me" (Brigham Young University devotional, Mar. 2, 1997), speeches.byu.edu.

24. Russell M. Nelson, "Revelation for the Church, Revelation for Our Lives," *Ensign,* May 2018, 95.

25. "Abide with Me!" *Hymns*, no. 166.

LOVE AS HE LOVES

One of the aspects of our Heavenly Father's plan of salvation that impresses me the most is the principle of love. Love is the greatest motivator. It is a powerful source of purpose, strength, and endurance as we go through our mortal experience. Because of our love for God and His love for us, He can enable us with His power to do things that we did not know we had the capacity to do.

The love Heavenly Father and Jesus Christ have for us explains much of why we are here in this world, why we have a mortal body, why we have to go through the sorrows and joys of mortality, why we have a Savior, why we will be resurrected one day, and why we will be eventually reunited with our heavenly parents.

Are you considering if that statement is true? If you are, then consider Doctrine and Covenants section 93, where our Lord,

Jesus Christ, gives us a beautiful promise: "Come unto the Father in my name, and *in due time receive of his fulness.* For if you keep my commandments you shall *receive of his fulness,* and be glorified in me as I am in the Father" (D&C 93:19–20; emphasis added).

We have been promised that if we keep the Lord's commandments, we will receive of the fulness of the Father. What does that fulness consist of?

We know that His fulness includes the greatest of all the gifts of God, eternal life (see D&C 14:7). With that comes godly qualities and attributes. God's capacity to feel love and to show love is one of His divine, eternal attributes. His perfect love is part of His fulness, part of that fulness we may receive in due time.

Adam and Eve were commanded to worship God and to love one another (see Moses 5:5, 8; 7:33). The Israelites were also commanded to love the Lord their God with all their heart, soul, and might and to love their neighbor.[1] They also received the Ten Commandments, which were given to them—and to us—to help them—and us—keep the commandments to love God and our neighbor. How do the Ten Commandments help us love God and our neighbor?

The commandments not to have other gods, not to make any graven image, not to take the name of God in vain, and to keep the Sabbath help us strengthen our relationship with God and increase our love for Him.

The commandments to honor our parents, not to kill, not to commit adultery, not to steal, not to bear false witness, and not to covet help us strengthen our relationship with others and increase our love for them.[2]

During His earthly ministry, Jesus Christ, in effect, summarized the Ten Commandments when someone asked Him:

"Master, which is the great commandment in the law? Jesus said unto him, Thou shalt *love* the Lord thy God with *all thy heart*, and with *all thy soul*, and with *all thy mind*. This is the first and great commandment. And the second is like unto it, Thou shalt *love* thy neighbour as thyself" (Matthew 22:36–39; emphasis added; see also Mark 12:28–31).

He also told His disciples: "A new commandment I give unto you, That *ye love* one another; *as I have loved you*, that ye also *love* one another" (John 13:34; emphasis added).

This divine teaching shows how important it is for us to learn to love God and our neighbor. We may ask ourselves:

- How do I do that?
- How do I *love the Lord my God* with all my heart, soul, and mind?
- How do I *love others* as myself and as Jesus Christ loves me?

One truth we learn from our questions is that to expand our capacity to love, we need to cultivate divine relationships. Our relationship with God and our righteous relationships with others are all divine, and they can help us become what we came to this earth to become. They can help us to be the best self each of us can be and to "[fill] the measure of [our] creation" (D&C 88:19; see also D&C 88:25).

So, what do we do? How do we cultivate relationships that are divine? Let me suggest some principles that may guide us.

First, follow the example of Jesus Christ. Jesus Christ is the perfect example of how to cultivate divine relationships. He has a close relationship with His Father, which is manifest in the way the Savior addresses His Father when He speaks to Him, in the way He respects and honors Him, and in the fact that He always wants to follow His Father's will. Jesus said, "For I came down from heaven, not to do mine own will, but the will of him that sent me" (John 6:38).

Jesus Christ also loves each of us, which is manifest in the way He approached those who came close to Him during His ministry on this earth and in the way we can feel His influence in our life when we turn to Him. He showed His love for His Father and for each of us when He offered Himself to be our Savior and when, through His Atonement, which included His suffering in Gethsemane, His Crucifixion on the cross, and His glorious Resurrection, He gave all of us access to eternal life.

President Ezra Taft Benson said: "We may never understand nor comprehend in mortality how [Jesus Christ] accomplished what He did, but we must not fail to understand why He did what He did. Everything He did was prompted by His unselfish, infinite love for us."[3]

We all have the potential to love, but to love someone specific, we need to have the desire to get to know him or her and we need to spend time together. Likewise, to love Heavenly Father and the Savior, we need to read the scriptures and the words of the prophets, who testify of Them; we need to pray with real intent; we need to fast; and we need to follow the commandments so our life can be aligned with God's will.

The same applies to our relationship with others; to develop love for someone, we need to have the desire to get to know them and we need to spend time with them, preferably face-to-face. We all need to develop friendships that will bring us blessings in the present and in the future.

Second, get out of your shell. As human beings, we tend to build a shell around ourselves. We may feel that we need to protect ourselves from harm. It is a natural behavior because we do not want to get hurt, either because we have been hurt in the past or we have seen others get hurt. Although we do need to protect ourselves and we need to discern between good and evil, I wonder if we go too far—to the point where we prefer to isolate ourselves instead of opening up for friendship and for love.

Elder Neal A. Maxwell said, "Though it may not be reciprocated, . . . love is never wasted."[4] This is so true. Every act of kindness has a positive effect, even if we do not see the results right away. Others can feel our good intentions, and even though they may not react the way we expect, in the end, goodness always brings more goodness.

If we spend too much time and effort building a shell around us, we run the risk of distancing ourselves from the influence of

God on our life and from the good influence that others may have on us. Being too comfortable inside our shell goes against the nature of the gospel of Jesus Christ; it goes against His doctrine. We did not come to this earth to be isolated.

We should not be afraid to show our vulnerabilities as guided by the Spirit. We are all vulnerable, and we need each other so we can overcome the vulnerabilities that we face in this mortal life. Many times, we can be the means through which Heavenly Father answers prayers, and most of the time, our prayers are answered through others.

Turn outward instead of inward. Turn to others so you can know them with their weaknesses and strengths and realize that you and they are not alone in your pains, in your struggles, and in your desires and efforts to get closer to God. We become stronger and we grow when we help others, and when we accept the help of others.

Give relationships enough time to grow and to give fruit. I feel that many of us "write off" other people after only a few minutes of interacting with them or after we catch them making one single mistake. Many of my best friends did not become my friends from the first interaction. In fact, when I look back, many of those friendships did not seem to start with strong compatibility.

Third, pray for that love and be patient. Fortunately, we are not alone in this quest to love at a higher level. We are all striving to develop such love, and to acquire it is a lifelong process. We are all learning to love; we are all learning to love better; we are all learning to love our Heavenly Father and our Savior with all our heart, soul, and might; and we are all learning to love others in a holier way.

Despite what the world may say, cultivating relationships is a decision—we decide whom we will put effort into and whom we will not. We can all use our agency to be more intentional in cultivating our divine relationships with God and our neighbor.

There is not a mold in which we all must fit. Each of us is different, and each of us has something important to contribute to God's work. As we keep our covenants with God, we will all write our own story, and, if we let Him, the Lord Jesus Christ will hold our hand as we are writing it.

Live according to the commandments of God; live so as to learn to follow the Holy Ghost; live knowing that you have a Father in Heaven, who loves you and who has a plan for you; live knowing that you have a Savior, who always has His arm stretched toward you and who is willing to take you by the hand and pull you up when you are down; live like you are alive; live like you have much to offer God and others; and live like others also have much to offer Him and you.

Please do not give up. Do not give up on your faith, do not give up on your efforts to live the commandments and to get closer to God, and do not give up on your efforts to develop love for others. Be patient with yourself and with the people around you.

The Savior is always ready to lift us up, every time we reach for Him. His grasp is strong enough to sustain us and to give us the strength to endure. His love is pure, perfect, abundant, and everlasting.

"Charity is the pure love of Christ, and it endureth forever; and whoso is found possessed of it at the last day, it shall be well with him [or her]. Wherefore, my beloved brethren [and sisters], pray unto the Father with all the energy of heart, that ye may be filled with this love, which he hath bestowed upon all who are true followers of his Son, Jesus Christ; that ye may become the sons [and daughters] of God; that when he shall appear we shall be like him, for we shall see him as he is; that we may have this hope; that we may be purified even as he is pure" (Moroni 7:47–48).

It is my prayer that we may continue cultivating our divine relationships with our Heavenly Father; our Savior, Jesus Christ; and our neighbor, so we may always have the Spirit of the Lord with us.

WE CAN REACH FOR THE SAVIOR WHEN WE EMULATE HIS WAY OF LOVING ALL OF GOD'S CHILDREN.

NOTES

1. See Leviticus 19:18; Deuteronomy 6:5; 10:12; 11:1; 19:9, 18; 30:6, 16, 20; Joshua 22:5.
2. See Exodus 20:1–17; Mosiah 13:12–24; Doctrine and Covenants 42:18–28; 59:5–24.
3. Ezra Taft Benson, "Jesus Christ: Our Savior and Redeemer," *Ensign*, Nov. 1983, 7.
4. Neal A. Maxwell, "A Brother Offended," *Ensign*, May 1982, 37.

LOOKING BACK

As I look back, I realize that my life, as it happens with each of us, has not been a bed of roses. There have been bumps, steep stretches, unexpected bends, and scary downhills. However, I can say with certainty that God's hand has always been guiding me when I have had the humility to acknowledge that I need His divine help at all times.

The greatest motivation I had for joining The Church of Jesus Christ of Latter-day Saints was my son Xavier and the immense love I felt for him. All I wanted was for him to be a good boy. At that point of my life, I was taking small steps of faith toward my Father in Heaven and my Savior Jesus Christ. Since then, They have shown me in many tangible and subtle ways that They love me and that They know me personally. I now have Carlos, who is my eternal companion and friend; I have two more children, Elena and Carlos Enrique; so far I have a daughter-in-law and three grandsons. I love all of them with all my heart and I rejoice in my posterity.

Because of His perfect love for us, all that our Heavenly Father expects from us is that we are good girls and good boys. He wants us to make sacred covenants with Him and to make a sincere effort to keep them. He wants us to love and trust Him; to hear His Son, our Savior, so we can receive His eternal gifts; and to love others as our Savior loves us.

I know that if we deny ourselves of all ungodliness and love God with all our might, mind, and strength, then Christ's grace is sufficient for us and we may be perfect in Him (see Moroni 10:32).

I also know that each of us individually and collectively can reach for the Savior and go forth to Him, with one accord, so He can heal every one of us and make us whole (see 3 Nephi 17:9–10).

WE CAN REACH FOR THE SAVIOR AS HE
REACHES FOR US IN PERFECT LOVE.